"I love Greg Gilbert's message fc
ues to struggle, for the believer v
gether, for the follower who has
said change is afoot and he will give you a hand, but it will
not be complete until the day of reckoning. So, stop worry-
ing. Read *Assured*, don't give up, and rest in your salvation."

Kyle Idleman, author of *Not a Fan* and *Don't Give Up*

"If you've been a Christian for any length of time, you've
asked the question. Perhaps you're haunted by it now. *How
do I really know I'm saved?* In this brilliant new book, Greg
Gilbert cuts through the fog of confusion surrounding our
questions—and fears—related to assurance. Bristling with
cinematic imagery and clear-eyed biblical reflection, *Assured*
will reanchor you on Christ, the solid rock. All other ground
is sinking sand."

Matt Smethurst, managing editor, The Gospel Coalition

"That fact that Christians are assured of salvation is one
of the greatest truths of God's Word, one of the most cher-
ished affirmations of the Reformation, and one of the central
pillars of the faithful Christian life. In this timely book,
Greg Gilbert, a tremendously gifted and faithful pastor-
theologian, presents a powerful case for assurance with deep
biblical and pastoral insight. The fact that Greg is my own
pastor just makes me all the more thankful for him—and
for this book."

R. Albert Mohler Jr, president,
the Southern Baptist Theological Seminary

ASSURED

ASSURED

DISCOVER GRACE,
LET GO OF GUILT, AND REST
IN YOUR SALVATION

GREG GILBERT

BakerBooks
a division of Baker Publishing Group
Grand Rapids, Michigan

© 2019 by Greg Gilbert

Published by Baker Books
a division of Baker Publishing Group
PO Box 6287, Grand Rapids, MI 49516-6287
www.bakerbooks.com

Printed in the United States of America

Library of Congress Cataloging-in-Publication Data
Names: Gilbert, Greg, 1977– author.
Title: Assured : discover grace, let go of guilt, and rest in your salvation / Greg Gilbert.
Description: Grand Rapids : Baker Publishing Group, 2019. | Includes bibliographical references.
Identifiers: LCCN 2018043301 | ISBN 9780801093227 (pbk.)
Subjects: LCSH: Assurance (Theology)
Classification: LCC BT785 .G55 2019 | DDC 234—dc23
LC record available at https://lccn.loc.gov/2018043301

19 20 21 22 23 24 25   7 6 5 4 3 2 1

To Matt—What a joy to be brothers
not only in this age but in the age to come!

Contents

The Problem of Assurance

Pastoral ministry has more than its fair share of both joy and heartbreak. On the one hand, there are moments and events that make you want to sing in praise to God—babies being born, wedding vows being exchanged, a dear brother or sister seeing God's hand move in a surprising way and their faith being strengthened because of it. Those are the beautiful moments, the ones that make pastoral ministry all worth it. But on the other hand, there are moments of deep sadness that make your heart cry out to God in an entirely different way—sitting with a couple who have just suffered their fourth miscarriage in three years, counseling someone through a cancer diagnosis or a job loss or the death of a loved one, reading the Bible quietly for the last time to a dear saint who's finally going home.

However, so far in my years of being a pastor, I haven't experienced anything more heartbreaking than watching the collapse of a professing Christian's faith. As I think about it, though, maybe *collapse* isn't quite the right word, because it's seldom dramatic or fast. You've probably seen internet videos of buildings undergoing a controlled demolition; it's quick and clean and streamlined and, in its own way, neat. The loss of faith isn't like that at all. If you've ever seen time-lapse video of an old tree slowly breaking down and decomposing, then you have a little better picture. When faith gives way to unbelief, there's no controlled explosion or neat collapse but rather just a slow, sometimes even imperceptible, *dwindling* until one day you look up and realize there's simply nothing left. Everything has been consumed.

Years ago, I watched that dwindling of faith happen in the life of a young man I'll call Trent. We couldn't have known it at the time, but he would turn out to be a classic example of the seed sown in the rocky soil from Jesus's parable of the sower—springing up in an explosion of apparent life but then quickly getting scorched by the sun and then withering. When Trent showed up at church, he was an excited and eager new Christian, and he looked like he was bound to grow into a spiritual warrior. He was theologically sharp, eager to spend time with other Christians, and, above all, a voracious reader. He read everything we as his pastors put in front of him—the Bible, books on theology and ecclesiology, devotional materials, commentaries, *everything*. Eventually, he met a wonderful young Christian woman in the church, and they married after a dating relationship that seemed to be a model of faithfulness and responsibility. Everything about Trent's spiritual life looked strong and true.

But that's when the trouble started. I don't remember exactly when the rot set in; even after all our conversations, I don't think Trent himself ever pinpointed it exactly. But our best guess is that Trent began to read a particular book (a good book, not a bad or heretical one) about what Christian joy ought to look like—how Christians should rejoice in their suffering, love Jesus, and find their joy in God's divine goodness—and he began to compare his own heart and mind and emotions to what he was reading. Of course, that's not necessarily a bad thing to do. In fact, it could actually be a good thing for a Christian to do and could very well result in a healthy encouragement to that Christian to loosen their heart's grasp on the pleasures of this world and cling more tightly to Christ. For Trent, though, the effect of comparing himself to the description in that book was dramatically different. Instead of being challenged to press on in faithfulness, Trent was terrified. Why? Because he didn't see in his own life the kind of joy that he read about in that book, and so he began to question whether he was really a Christian at all.

From there, the corrosion deepened rapidly. Over the next few months, Trent fell into a hopeless vortex of introspection and self-judgment. No matter how often or how fervently we exhorted him to look to Christ and find peace in the gospel, Trent lost his footing. In the end, he simply declared that he couldn't possibly be a Christian because he didn't have the joy or the passionate love for Jesus that a Christian ought to have, and he left the church and ultimately the faith.

Don't get me wrong. Of course not every Christian's wrestling with assurance is the same as Trent's, and thank God not every Christian's struggle ends so catastrophically either. But I'm also quite sure that Trent's struggle with the question "Am I a Christian, *really*?" is one that dogs many Christians, if not *every* Christian, at one point or another

13

in their lives. I say that not just as a truism or a throwaway hunch but as the considered fruit of dozens of conversations I've had across coffee shop tables about this very issue. I'm sure the coffee joints in Louisville don't know it, but they've made a *ton* of money from me talking with people over the years about assurance of salvation!

I wish I could say that the questions people have, and the doubts with which they struggle, are all the same. That would make it easy for me as a pastor. Then I could fix that *one* biblical misunderstanding, answer that *one* theological question, and all would be well. But the questions and doubts are never exactly the same, and they are almost never simple. Sometimes, yes, a person's struggle with assurance is born of a particular unanswered theological question, and it's wonderful to be able to answer that question and watch everything begin to fall into place. But sometimes a lack of assurance is far more complicated than one specific unanswered question. Sometimes it's more emotional than rational. Sometimes it's born of a whole theological worldview that's off by just a few catastrophic degrees. Sometimes there's no identifiable reason for it at all, and a person is just gripped by an existential dread that they will prove to be, as the old confessions put it, a "superficial professor."

To me, the question of assurance of salvation—or, to be more precise, the lack of assurance—is a particularly unwelcome, terrifying, and even surprising presence in the Christian experience, like the black-robed figure at Prince Prospero's ball. After all, at its heart Christianity claims to be all about certainties, not questions or doubts. We *know* Jesus is the Son of God; we *know* he died on the cross as a ransom for many; we *know* he was resurrected from the grave; and we *know* he offers forgiveness to everyone who trusts in him. Our entire worldview is built on certainties, both historical and theological, and that's what sets Christianity apart from most other religions of the world. They have questions; Christianity has answers. They have enigmas; Christianity has truths. They explore; Christianity declares.

What's more, the biblical authors themselves write with a rock-solid sense of certainty that seems to go deeper than that particular things actually happened. Their certainty appears to be not just historical but existential, even *personal.* They seem confident about not only the facts of Christianity but also those facts' redemptive significance, and they seem sure that they themselves have been swept up in that redemption. What's more, these authors even seem to expect their own certainty to translate to other believers as well. They write as if they want *you* and *me* to be certain about our faith too. Thus, the apostle John says in his first letter, "I write these things to you who believe in the name of the Son of God, that you may *know* that you have eternal life" (1 John 5:13, emphasis added). Paul too writes, "For I am *sure* that neither death nor life, nor angels nor rulers, nor things present nor things to come, nor powers, nor height nor depth, nor anything else in all creation, will be able to separate us from the love of God in Christ Jesus our Lord" (Rom. 8:38–39, emphasis added). And the author of Hebrews speaks of God's oath and promise as "a sure and steadfast *anchor* of the soul" (Heb. 6:19, emphasis added). There's not much room for doubt, is there? The language is strong and solid: "that you may *know*"; "I am *sure*"; a "steadfast *anchor*." The whole atmosphere of the Bible is not one of doubt but rather of an assurance so strong that it can declare in the words of Job: "I *know* that my Redeemer lives" (Job 19:25, emphasis added).

But if that's the case, then what is this dark, horrifying figure of doubt that glides through the experience of so many Christians, quieting the rejoicing and delight of assurance? Where does it come from? And why do so many Christians find it so difficult to say with John, with Paul, and with the author of Hebrews, "I know. I am sure. I have this as a sure and steadfast anchor of my soul"? Those are some of the questions I want to tackle with you in this book. Before we start, though, I should be straightforward: you're not going to walk away from reading this book with some silver bullet that will put an end to doubt altogether. Why? Because there's no such bullet. Nor is there any faithful theological construct or pat answer that will expel the black-robed figure from the party once and for all. We are finite creatures, with limited minds and dependent souls. In some shape or form, doubt will always be part of our experience, and the search for assurance will always be a fight until the day we stand with Christ and our faith is turned to sight.

But even so, take heart. Because whether you realize it now or not, doubt can be tamed. It can be resisted. It can be brought to its knees. In fact, it may surprise you to find out that doubt can even become, ironically, one of the means God uses to deepen your faith in and dependence on Jesus, to drive you back to the cross and to a desperate trust in Christ. Ultimately, my hope for you as we consider doubt and assurance together in this book is not so much that doubt will vanish entirely, but that as you understand more deeply the architecture of Christian assurance, doubt will begin to lose some of its destructive power in your life and maybe even drive you to cling more tightly to Christ as your only hope of salvation.

None of that, of course, is easy. Thus, you're reading a *book* about this topic rather than a blog post or a tweet. The topic of Christian assurance has always been a difficult one, and complexities are on every side. For one thing, a few passages of Scripture just seem *designed* to unsettle us, to make us question whether we are really saved, really included in God's promises of eternal life. Take 2 Corinthians 13:5–6 for example: "Examine yourselves, to see whether you are in the faith. Test yourselves. Or do you not realize this about yourselves, that Jesus Christ is in you?—unless indeed you fail to meet the test!" Wait a second . . . "Unless indeed you fail to meet the test"? How can that possibly square with a rock-solid assurance that I'm saved? Then there are the famous (or infamous) warning passages, especially from Hebrews. Sentences such as "It is impossible, in the case of those who . . . have fallen away, to restore them again to repentance" (Heb. 6:4, 6) and "It is a fearful thing to fall into the hands of the living God" (Heb. 10:31) leave many Christians with more fear than confidence, and sometimes even terrified that they might have lost their salvation.

Even beyond specific biblical texts, the topic of assurance has proved to be a treacherous road, theologically speaking. There are so many ways to go wrong. For example, some Christians throughout history have simply thrown up their hands and declared that there can be no assurance of salvation at all. Sometimes that assertion has been largely epistemological in nature—that is, we can't *know* finally if we are indeed saved. But other times it's been a more objective assertion that we can in fact lose the salvation we once had.

ASSURED

Even among those with a strong doctrine of the preservation of the saints, though, exactly *how* Christians can come to any sense of assurance has been a thorny question. In the pursuit of assurance, we can easily run off the road and into two opposite errors—legalism or antinomianism. If we are of a legalist bent, then we tend to gain assurance of our salvation through a focus on our own works, which is inherently dangerous because our assurance can subtly become a matter of putting faith in our works rather than in Jesus. Conversely, if we tend toward an *antinomian* spirit (a word meaning literally "against law"), we'll discount good works entirely as a confirmation of salvation and find ourselves in danger of presuming on the grace of the King. Both of those pitfalls— legalism and antinomianism—must be avoided if we're to have a deep, solid, and biblical assurance of salvation.

But let's be honest. For most of us, the question of assurance isn't on our minds because of a particular theological construct or even because we're just curious about a passage of Scripture we happened to run across. It's on our minds because of our sin. We look at our lives and see the sin that still exists in us, and we wonder if a true Christian's life and heart can really look like *that*. For some, the issue is that we don't see the growth in holiness that we'd like to see, even over time. For others, it's that we don't experience the victory we'd like to have over a particular sin. And for still others (like Trent), it's that the fruit, joy, praise, patience, and love we *think* ought to mark a Christian simply don't seem to mark us—at least as far as we can tell. And so we fear, or sometimes even despair.

So, in the midst of all those complexities and difficulties, how do you find assurance? And is it even possible? Well,

I think it is, and I think the Bible says it is too. In fact, I think the Bible teaches that assurance—to some degree or another—is the new birthright inheritance of every Christian and is even inherent to the nature of faith. Yes, some Christians will experience a deeper and more settled assurance than others. And yes, one's sense of assurance will ebb and flow through the circumstances and years of life. But assurance isn't like the pot of gold at the end of a rainbow, as if it's a treasure only a few Christians enjoy. No, it's like John explained: "I write these things *to you who believe in the name of the Son of God*, that you may know that you have eternal life" (1 John 5:13, emphasis added). He did not write to undercut assurance but to *establish* and *strengthen* it. And he wanted to do that for *all* who believe, not just some.

Our aim in this book is to explore the biblical idea of Christian assurance and to ask questions like the following:

- What does the Bible teach is the right foundation of Christian assurance?
- What role do our good works play in our assurance?
- What lies do we tend to believe that undermine assurance?
- How do we go wrong in considering our good works?
- How do we strengthen assurance or even regain it if it's been lost?

For the next several chapters, then, our first task will be simply to explore together the architecture of Christian assurance—that is, how the Bible seeks to assure Christians of their salvation in Christ. I believe the Bible reveals four main sources of assurance: the gospel of Jesus Christ, the promises of God, the witness of the Spirit, and the fruits of obedience. As we tap into them, these four realities—each in its own way and together in harmony with one another—create a sense of confidence and certainty in our hearts that we are in fact children of God and heirs of eternal life. Here's the problem, though, and the reason many Christians find their assurance fails to launch: these four sources of assurance don't function in exactly the same way in our lives, and we aren't even meant to treat them all in the same way. So, what do I mean by that?

The best way to think about it is that two of these sources of assurance—the gospel of Jesus Christ and the promises of God—are held out by Scripture as *driving* sources of assurance. In other words, they are the ultimate fountainheads from which our sense of certainty of our salvation erupts, and the deeper we press into them with understanding and faith, the greater our sense of assurance will be. As for the fruits of obedience (our good works as Christians), they seem to be held out by Scripture not as a driving source of assurance but as a *confirming* source of assurance—that is, not one in which we should put our faith but one that can nevertheless serve to confirm our sense that we really are children of God or, alternatively, provide a warning that our sense of assurance is actually a false one. Finally, the witness of the Spirit is best described as a *supernatural* source of assurance, a gift from God by which the Holy Spirit gives birth directly in our souls to a deep and profound sense of comfort, security, and assurance.

Perhaps an analogy will help us understand the difference between *driving*, *confirming*, and *supernatural* sources of assurance. Obviously, no analogy is perfect, but this one goes some distance in helping distinguish especially between a driver and a confirmer (or indicator) of assurance. Consider this: In the design of a car, there is a profound difference between a driver of speed and a confirmer of speed, between the accelerator and the speedometer. If we want the car to go faster, we push on the accelerator; we put weight on it, and the car goes. Now, of course, when we do that, one of the results is that the speedometer on the dashboard *indicates*, or *shows*, or *confirms* that the car is going. But the speedometer is a sign of speed, not the source of speed. If we want more speed, we can't just raise our hand to the dashboard and use our fingers to push the needle up and expect the car to go faster. To get speed, you have to focus on and put weight on the source of speed, not the indicator of speed. So what then, you might ask, is the point of having a speedometer in the first place? Well, a speedometer can show us very quickly if we are rightly putting weight on the accelerator in the first place. If the speedometer reads "0," then chances are our foot isn't on the accelerator at all.

Maybe you can already see how this applies to the question of assurance. If we want to get more and stronger assurance, the way to do that is not to fiddle with the indicator—that is, to make sure we do a few more good works and fewer bad ones so that we'll feel more worthy of heaven. This is an important point because, sadly, it's exactly how many Christians react to a lack of assurance. Because that sense of doubt and fear is often caused by seeing their own sin, they think the solution is therefore to focus on their sin, or their good works, or their lack of good works—which, of course, is ultimately to focus on self rather than on God. But if that's the way we react to a lack of assurance, we might as well think that the way to respond to a lack of speed in our car is to fiddle with the speedometer! But that's absurd. The way to respond to a lack of assurance is to focus on and put weight on the driving sources of assurance—the promises of God and the gospel of Jesus Christ. As we do so, the result will be a greater confidence of our salvation *and* an increase in the kind of godly life and works that indicate true salvation.

Here's another analogy that might help. The fruit on a tree can be an indicator of the tree's health, but to achieve a healthier tree, the solution isn't to make the fruit look better. Rather, it's to tend to the root, which drives and creates the tree's health. In the same way, the fruit of our lives can be an important indicator of our spiritual health, but we won't be able to increase our sense of assurance and confidence in our salvation simply by trying to make that fruit look better. Duct-taping apples to a sick tree or painting rotten apples red doesn't make the tree healthier. No, we have to tend to the root, and then the fruit—the indicator of health—will improve.

And what about the witness of the Spirit, the *supernatural* source of assurance? Well, every analogy breaks down at some point, and this is that point. I'm afraid the witness of the Spirit—something God imparts directly and supernaturally to a believer's heart—doesn't have a nice analogue in our image of the car. At best, we might think of it as a mostly unexpected nitro-shot of speed delivered directly from heaven! But the point is, when the Lord decides to give a believer an unusual sense of comfort and assurance, it is a beautiful and immensely valuable gift—and it usually comes most powerfully right when it's needed most.

So, this seems to be the architecture of Christian assurance. Our confidence that we really are saved is grounded in and founded on an abiding trust that Jesus saves sinners and that the Father will honor his Son by keeping his promises. Meanwhile, our good works (or lack thereof) act to confirm that we really are saved or warn that something is not right so that we may react accordingly. And God, by his Holy Spirit, imparts a precious, deep, and sometimes profound sense to our souls of our redemption and adoption as his children.

It probably won't be surprising that this architecture of assurance reflects the theological architecture of salvation itself. Consider this representative passage from Titus 3:4–8:

> But when the goodness and loving kindness of God our Savior appeared, he saved us, not because of works done by us in righteousness, but according to his own mercy, by the washing of regeneration and renewal of the Holy Spirit, whom he poured out on us richly through Jesus Christ our Savior, so that being justified by his grace we might become heirs according to the hope of eternal life. The saying is trustworthy, and I want you to insist on these things, so that those who have believed in God may be careful to devote themselves to good works.

Paul makes two statements here about good works. The first is that good works *are not* the basis of, or reason for, or grounds for, or cause of our salvation. "He saved us," Paul writes, "not because of works done by us in righteousness, but according to his own mercy." The second, though, is that once we have believed and thus become heirs of eternal life, we should "be careful to devote [ourselves] to good works." Now, most Christians recognize immediately the importance of those two statements to the question of salvation: we are not saved by works but rather works flow from salvation. In other words, the correct order is salvation, then works. In fact, if we get that order backward—if we conceive the order as "works, then salvation"—we've turned the entire gospel on its head. That theological architecture, so to speak, is key to rightly understanding salvation.

Well, the same architecture seems to hold not only when it comes to getting saved but also when it comes to being assured of our salvation. If we want to increase or build our sense of confidence in our own salvation, the way to do that is to press into our faith and trust in the Triune God's unbreakable promises in the gospel of Jesus Christ, *not* just to do more good deeds so we'll be able to say, "Whew! Now I feel good about myself." To do that would actually be to shift our faith, our confidence, and our reliance from Jesus to self.

Our goal in the next few chapters is to better understand the sources of our assurance—the gospel of Jesus Christ, the promises of God, the witness of the Spirit, and the fruits of obedience. Along the way, we'll consider a few specific lies we tend to believe, untruths about God and the gospel that slowly but profoundly corrode our assurance. We'll also consider some specific ways we tend to *misuse* the indicator of good works and how to take care that we use the indicator of good works *rightly*, as the Bible intends, and not in a way that wrongly undermines assurance or (even worse!) shifts our faith from Jesus to our own works. Finally, near the end of the book we'll turn to some practical questions—how to think about what Christians have called "besetting sins" and what we can do to strengthen our assurance or even regain it if it's been lost.

So, that's where we're headed. I don't know exactly why you picked up this book and began to read it, but my guess is that it's because you want to have a deep and strong sense of confidence that the blessings of salvation in Christ really are yours. Maybe you're not struggling with any particular crisis of doubt. If that's true, then I hope this book will encourage you to focus again on the promises of the Triune God, help you rejoice even more about his goodness toward you, and spur you on to even greater love and good deeds.

However, maybe picking up this book was, for you, an act tinged with urgency. After all, it's one thing to read a book about assurance when you're feeling quite settled in your faith; it's another thing entirely to do so when your heart is full of doubt and fear. Friend, if that's how you feel, then I want you to understand me clearly right from the start: this book is for you. I'm convinced that our kind and loving Lord intends for us to live this Christian life not in a perpetual sense of worry and fear but rather with joy and love and godly determination to run the race well—and ultimately with a delight-filled *confidence* that what waits for us at the end is his strong embrace. My hope is that by the time we finish thinking about this topic together, a new spark of hope and certainty and confidence and assurance will be burning in your heart, lit by a renewed focus on and treasuring of God's promises in the gospel. I hope you'll also be better equipped to biblically and faithfully tend to your own sense of assurance—recognizing the lies that most tend

25

to undermine your confidence and learning how to use an assessment of your life and works to spur you on in the faith.

"I write these things," John says, "that you may know that you have eternal life" (1 John 5:13). That's the goal. Now, let's get started!

The Driving Sources of Assurance

The Gospel of Jesus Christ

I have a teenage son who plays basketball. So far he's not a very big guy, but he's developed enough skill at the game that he's usually able to contribute in a big way. Still, though, even a "skillz player," as he calls himself, would benefit from not having opponents tower head and shoulders over him. You can dribble between a bigger guy's legs only so many times before he gets wise to the trick!

Recently, my son's coach recommended that he start going to the gym and lifting some light weights. So, occasionally my son has been accompanying me to the gym where I'm a member and doing workouts with me. But here's the thing: my son isn't a member of the gym. When we walk up to the desk, *I'm* the one who calls up the membership information on my smartphone and buzzes us into the gym. And when

I do, I point to my son and explain that he's with me, and the attendant nods and waves us through. Once that's done, though, my son is free to do anything I'm free to do in the gym. Whatever equipment I'm authorized to use by virtue of my paid membership, he's authorized to use because he's there with me. Whatever privileges I have to use the locker room, the pool, the weights, the basketball court, he shares them all *because he's with me*. I have access to the gym by right of a paid membership; he has access to it not at all by right but by virtue of his relationship with me. You see? My son's right to be present in the gym and take advantage of its resources is no less real or valid than mine. It's just based on a different foundation—not his own paid membership but his father's.

What does all this have to do with assurance of salvation? Everything in the world. Take a look at Hebrews 10:19–22:

> Therefore, brothers, since we have confidence to enter the holy places by the blood of Jesus, by the new and living way that he opened for us through the curtain, that is, through his flesh, and since we have a great priest over the house of God, let us draw near with a true heart in full assurance of faith, with our hearts sprinkled clean from an evil conscience and our bodies washed with pure water.

This passage is all about having access to the presence of God—that is, having a right to stand before him. Thus, the author of Hebrews writes that we as Christians should "have confidence" to enter into God's presence, and we should "draw near" to him not with an "evil conscience"—that is, with fear that we don't belong or that we'll be cast out—but "in full assurance of faith." That's the goal—to stand in the presence of God and enjoy his blessings with full assurance and confidence that we *belong* there.

But did you see how that kind of assurance and confidence is created? It would have been easy enough for the author to write, "We draw near with the confidence of a paid membership, with the full assurance that we've done what's necessary to earn access to the presence of God." But he didn't write that. In fact, in quick succession the author mentions three reasons why we can have this kind of confident assurance to stand in God's presence without fear. First, we have this confidence "by the blood of Jesus"; second, "by the new and living way that he opened for us through the curtain"; and third, because "we have a great priest over the house of God." All three of those reasons for confidence—Christ's blood, the torn curtain of the temple, and Christ's role as great priest—have to do with Jesus's death in the place of his people. Do you see the point the author of Hebrews is making? Our confidence and assurance that we can enter God's presence—that we can in fact stand before him with no fear of being thrown out—are actually *created* by our recognizing that our access to him is based *not at all* on anything in us or about us but rather on Jesus Christ's work *for* us.

This is a critical point to grasp in our fight for assurance. Most Christians would readily affirm that our right to enter the presence of God, to draw near to him, was won for us by Christ in his life, death, and resurrection. That's not what causes our problems. Our trouble begins when we ask, "Well, okay, but how can I draw near to God *in confidence, with full assurance?*" And for many of us, the answer that lurks in the back of our minds is that even if Jesus has brought us into the presence of God, we dare not enjoy being there, or have any assurance of the appropriateness of our being there, or have any sense of the safety and rightness of our being there unless we now earn it ourselves. *Jesus may have gotten us here*, we think, *but now we need to prove we belong.*

But do you see how these verses from Hebrews 10 cut hard against that way of thinking? The blood of Jesus doesn't barely sneak us into the presence of God; it actually gives us every right in the universe to be there—and to be there with confidence and joy. And therefore the work of Christ on our behalf actually creates confidence and assurance; it is a *source* of assurance. The more we understand it, embrace it, and cherish it, the greater our sense of confidence and assurance will be. The fact is, our minds and hearts will always look for a way to find *self*-assurance. More than anything, we desperately want to justify our presence before God's throne, to show the universe and maybe God himself that even if we're saved by grace, God ultimately made a good choice. We want to make it clear that we belong, and *then* we'll stand in God's presence with confidence. But the author of Hebrews rules that kind of thinking right out of bounds. We *should* stand in God's presence with confidence and assurance, he says, but not because we've paid our own dues or proved our own mettle. We stand there with confidence solely because of what Jesus has done for us. Our confidence that we belong in the presence of God is not *self*-confidence; it's *Christ*-confidence.

In fact, the whole tenor of the gospel message is designed to undermine and destroy self-assurance. Paul gets right at this in Romans 3:27 when he asks, "Then what becomes of our boasting?" And his answer: "It is excluded." Boasting is the natural and expected fruit of self-assurance. If we think we stand in God's presence by our own right, it's entirely natural that we should smack our chest and say, "I did this!" But according to Paul, the gospel—right down to its root—is hostile to that kind of self-assurance.

In fact, so hostile is the gospel to self-assurance that every individual component of the gospel message wages war against it. Consider this first: one of the most important things to understand about the gospel is that it is a message. Translate the Greek word for "gospel," *euangelion*, and you get, literally, "good news," a message that brings joy. And what is that message? It is that although we are sinners before our Creator God, he has acted in love to send his Son to live and die and rise again in our place so that if we put our faith and trust in him, we too will rise right along with him—first to newness of life and ultimately to life eternal. So, the gospel is news. It's a message, and every last piece of that message is a full-frontal assault on self-assurance. Let's see how.

How Our Sin against Our Creator God Assaults Self-Assurance

The first component of the gospel is its declaration that we are sinners before God. That's obviously not good news, but it sets the dark context against which the good news comes. But here's the point: the fact that we are sinners cuts deeply against any tendency we have to feel self-assured, but we'll never see that until we understand exactly what sin really is and just how deeply offensive it is to God. One of the greatest misunderstandings Christians often have is not realizing

31

just how awful sin really is. And ironically, it turns out that an inadequate understanding of sin—a failure to realize just how catastrophically and completely we have made ourselves a stench in God's nostrils—will ultimately cause our sense of assurance to corrode and weaken.

How so? Because if we don't understand just how hopelessly evil and pervasive our sin is, then we will begin to think that we can fix it, cure it, wipe it off the surface of our lives and present to God something he will be proud of. But the Bible teaches exactly the opposite. Sin is not something superficial but something awful. It is not something easily fixed but something that stains us to the core and cries out for eternal justice. The way we often think of sin and the way the Bible speaks of it are wholly different. We think we can cure sin; Scripture says it's an incurable wound. We think we can wipe sin off the surface of our lives; Scripture says it goes all the way to our hearts. We think our sin is just a mistake, a "missing of the mark"; Scripture says it's high-handed rebellion against God. We think we can try a little harder and clean ourselves up enough to slip into God's party; Scripture says we are by nature children of wrath who deserve to be cast out of his presence forever.

But here's the upshot of all this: because we have such a low, benign, toothless, and *false* understanding of sin, we wind up convincing ourselves that self-salvation and self-assurance might really be possible. But it is precisely that false hope in self-salvation that ultimately destroys our assurance.

Here's how. If we think of our sin as something that exists more or less on the surface of our lives, something that can be cleaned up relatively easily with enough willpower, moral fortitude, and righteous determination, then we'll be sorely tempted to give self-assurance a try. We'll become convinced that if we just do a little more of this or a little less of that, then we'll eventually reach a level of moral rectitude that will justify our presence in God's court. But the fatal error in that thinking, of course, is that over and over again that cliff jump toward self-assurance fails because sin *isn't* just a little mistake that can be cleaned up and wiped off our otherwise pretty good lives. It's a rebellion against God—a brokenness, corruption, and guilt that goes all the way to our core—that deserves hell. So time and again, we find ourselves taking the leap toward self-assurance but failing because we run smack into the reality of our own intractable and hell-deserving sin. And when we look up from the dirt, our sin stares us in the face with an evil I-told-you-so grin, and we fall again into doubt and fear about whether we really have a right to be in God's presence at all. Our attempts at *self*-assurance fail us, and so we find ourselves with no assurance at all.

But consider what happens instead when we think of sin like the Bible does—not as a minor problem we can solve with a little extra effort but as a catastrophic failure we can *never* solve. Then when we look at our sin apart from Christ and his gospel, what we'll feel is not hopeful moral determination but rather abject hopelessness. "The wages of sin is death," Paul writes in Romans 6:23. "Your iniquities have made a separation between you and your God," Isaiah writes in Isaiah 59:2. "The soul who sins," Ezekiel writes, "shall die" (Ezek. 18:20).

Pretty bleak. And yet the glorious irony of the gospel is that it's precisely from the soil of that kind of hopelessness that hope—and ultimately assurance—springs. When we realize that self-salvation is impossible and self-assurance is simply not an option, that's when we begin to look around for a Savior. And when we find that Savior in Jesus, we will never again jump hopelessly into the void in an attempt to reach a moral plateau of acceptability we'll never be able to reach. We will make no more doomed-to-fail attempts at proving ourselves worthy to be in God's presence. Instead, we'll cling to Jesus. We'll hear his promise that we have full access to God, *but only by his blood*, and we'll find that his promise (unlike the promise of self-assurance) is never-failing. And therefore we will rest.

Incidentally, this biblical understanding of sin's true evil and incurability shows me with crystal clarity the falsehood of the idea that a true Christian can lose their salvation. Of course, this isn't the only thing that convinces me of that! The Bible is full of passages that make it clear that Jesus will never lose those who come to him in faith. But still, here's my point: If you think you can commit a sin so bad that your salvation would be lost, I want to know why you think you haven't already committed it. I want to know why you think you're not committing it right now. In fact, I want to know why you think your sin isn't bad enough—at every minute of every hour of every day—to completely undermine and overwhelm your salvation. You see my point? If you think you can lose your salvation if you sin, and if you think you're not losing it even at this very moment, then your understanding of the sin that *right now* stains you to the very core is flawed and inadequate. Why? Because the Bible teaches that our sin is so pervasive, so deep, and so awful that if our salvation could be lost because of it, we'd all lose our salvation every minute of every day.

I hope you can see the deep irony in all this. Our normal way of thinking tells us that if we could just convince ourselves that sin is not so bad, that we can do things to excuse and fix it, then that would give us cause for a sense of assurance; then we'd have hope of being able to beat it, to win. But what the Bible actually teaches is that true assurance grows from an abject realization of our hopelessness. Why? Because that hopelessness drives us to Jesus, who is infinitely trustworthy and therefore a solid foundation for assurance. As long as we think of sin as a tough but ultimately conquerable challenge, we'll keep trying and trying and failing to reach the point where we feel worthy enough to be in God's presence. It's only when we realize that those efforts are hopeless—that we are dead in our trespasses and sins, not just a little sick—that we'll run to Jesus and find the *only* legitimate way for us to draw near to God. And so, by his blood alone, we will finally stand there in joy and confident assurance.

How Christ's Work for Us Assaults Self-Assurance

We said in the last section that the very depth and evil of our sin—our rebellion against God—cuts the root of self-assurance. But you probably noticed that it's not the evil of sin considered alone that creates confidence and the full assurance of faith. It's that the horrific evil of our sin and the sheer hopelessness of our situation drive us to Jesus, in whose blood we finally find an abiding confidence and assurance.

Of course, the very nature of Christ's work on our behalf launches yet another assault on our tendency toward self-assurance. Why? Because what he did for us was not a matter of working *with* us to pull us out of our predicament. It wasn't a 50-50 cooperation between us and him, or even 90-10. What he did for us, he did *for* us, without our help or input or contribution. Remember that truth, rest in it, and you'll further cut the root of self-assurance and begin to grow in your heart the "full assurance of faith."

The apostle Paul addresses this very thing in Romans 5. This is what he writes:

> Therefore, since we have been justified by faith, we have peace with God through our Lord Jesus Christ. Through him we have also obtained access by faith into this grace in which we stand, and we rejoice in hope of the glory of God. . . . For while we were still weak, at the right time Christ died for the ungodly. For one will scarcely die for a righteous person—though perhaps for a good person one would dare even to die—but God shows his love for us in that while we were still sinners, Christ died for us. (vv. 1–2, 6–8)

Did you notice the idea of access there again? This time it's access into "this grace in which we stand," but the idea is the same as it was in Hebrews 10. We stand in God's presence justified and welcomed, and we have full access to and enjoyment of all the blessings of his presence and of eternity. But notice again how Paul says we have obtained this access into grace. It's not by our own efforts or our own moral victories. It's "through him," that is, "through our Lord Jesus Christ."

So, how exactly has that happened? It has happened because "Christ died." Now, of course, as Christians, we all know this; it's the heart of the gospel. But look how Paul describes those for whom Christ died. His language is nothing short of brutal. They are "weak," "ungodly," and "sinners." To make matters worse, he even contrasts them with a hypothetical "righteous" or "good" person. Look what Paul is saying here. Weak, ungodly, unrighteous, no-good sinners—that's who Christ died for. Which means that if you're a Christian, that's *you*. And that's not exactly fertile soil for self-assurance, is it? Once we understand what the Bible says we were before Christ, we'll start to despair (in the most gloriously joyful way) of ever proving ourselves worthy of his love or somehow deserving of his work on our behalf.

The problem, though, is that we don't easily think of ourselves that way. More than anything, we want to think that we contributed at least *something* to anything we have. So, "the full assurance of faith" that comes from relying entirely on Christ and not at all on ourselves requires doing some hard work of convincing our own hearts of the utter *solitude* of Christ's work for us: We did not contribute to it or cooperate with it. We had in fact no hand in it at all.

This is in fact where the heart of the Christian gospel lies: When a person believes in Christ, a stunning trade takes place between that believer and Jesus. Our sinful, unrighteous, weak, ungodly life is transferred and credited to him, and he died because of it. And at the same time, his perfect, spotless, always-righteous life is transferred and credited to us, and we live because of it. Martin Luther once described this trade between Christ and the believer as a "wonderful exchange":

> By a wonderful exchange our sins are no longer ours but Christ's, and the righteousness of Christ not Christ's but

ours. He has emptied Himself of His righteousness that He might clothe us with it, and fill us with it. And He has taken our evils upon Himself that He might deliver us from them.[1]

This truth—that Christ died not for the godly or the acceptable or even the barely tolerable, but for the ungodly—assaults our innate desire to leap toward self-assurance. That's good, because the bent of our prideful hearts is always to try to make ourselves worthy of what Christ has done for us, to show him that he made a good choice in acting to save us and that his return on investment will be spectacular—or at least not embarrassing. The trouble, though, is that we'll simply never get to that level. And therefore every time we try, we'll always fall short and go slinking into a corner wondering if Jesus is sorry he made the effort. But once we accept that Christ died for us *while we were still sinners*, while we were nothing short of ungodly, we can rest in the knowledge that our access to God isn't dependent on us at all. Our welcome into the throne room of heaven isn't in the least because of anything in us or about us. It is because of Jesus—completely, entirely, and without qualification or exception. *Through him* we have obtained access into this grace in which we stand.

What does this mean for you if your sense of confidence and assurance of salvation are weak? Well, at least part of the trouble may be that you're trying—and failing—to prove to yourself and maybe even to God that you're worthy of the salvation Jesus has given you. And every time you fail in that effort (which is *every time!*), you spiral into a vortex of despair that makes you think, *Well, if I'm not worthy of it, then it must not be mine.* But, friend, don't you see that your abject, hopeless, jaw-dropping *unworthiness* is precisely the point of the gospel? Grace is by definition undeserved, unpaid for, unmerited, and unwarranted. So, give it some thought. Maybe part of what you need to do is stop trying so hard to *merit* grace and start focusing instead on the One who acted in love to save you even though you were—and are—a hopeless wreck of an ungodly sinner. He knows it all, dear friend, and he loves you and acted to save you anyway.

Maybe for you, though, the situation is slightly different. Maybe it's not so much that you can't quite seem to do enough to feel worthy of salvation but rather that you're afraid you've already *disqualified* yourself from salvation— that your past is full of too much garbage for God ever to forgive you. Maybe you're paralyzed by guilt. Well, consider this: Do you know what gives guilt its power? It's fear and embarrassment—a desire by the guilty person to run and hide from what they did. And so do you know how to disarm guilt in your life, how to find rest and confidence in Jesus even in the harsh glare of your sin? The solution is ironic, but it's true: stop hiding from it! Stop trying to avoid its accusations, and instead stare it in the face and agree with it about how horrible you are. When Satan or another person or even your own mind accuses you of sin and tells you how awful you are and how unworthy you are of God's love, don't argue! Don't say, "No, please don't bring that up. I can't bear to think about it." And don't defend yourself either. Don't say, "Well, there were these mitigating circumstances around that one, and I was really tired that day, and besides, all these good things over here balance it out." And above all, don't say, "Okay, okay, you're right. But give me time, and I'll make it up. Let me have another shot, and this time

I'll do better!" Instead, just agree with the accuser and say, "Yes, I did all that; I *am* all that. I am an unrighteous, weak, ungodly sinner who is utterly unworthy of God's love and grace. And yet Christ died for the ungodly! Christ died for ungodly *me*."

Listen, your access to God is not dependent on you being worthy of it, and it's not dependent on you doing something to win it. Your access to God is cemented open by the gracious, undeserved, unmerited work of Christ on your behalf—and that's all. So, let go of the impossible desire to make Christ's death for you *worth it*. When you do, you'll start to enjoy the deep, comforting assurance of knowing that in fact you could *never* be worth it—and yet he died for you anyway.

How the Nature of Faith Assaults Self-Assurance

If it's true that we are hopeless and helpless rebels against God, and if it's true that Jesus has done everything necessary to win our salvation, then what's the response that's required from us? Most Christians know the answer to that question. It's faith. *Faith*, or *belief*, is one of those words that's embedded in Christianity's very core. Theologians say our justification before God is by faith alone, and Paul writes that the righteousness of God comes "through faith in Jesus Christ for all who believe" (Rom. 3:22). In the passage we just considered from Romans 5, he writes that we "have also obtained access *by faith* into this grace in which we stand" (v. 2, emphasis added).

So the instrument by which we appropriate or take hold of the salvation that Christ won through his life and word—our appropriate response to the gospel—is faith. Now, as Christians, we often take that fact for granted. It seems obvious to us, and it's hard for us to imagine that the means of taking hold of salvation could have been something else. But why couldn't it have been? Why couldn't God have declared that salvation would be by *something else* alone? Maybe love alone or kindness alone or good works alone. Of all the virtues God could have chosen to be the instrument of salvation, why did he choose faith?

The answer to that question is fascinating, and it also launches another assault on our tendency toward self-assurance. To put it simply, the reason God chose faith to be the instrument of our salvation instead of some other virtue is that faith isn't a virtue at all!

Let's think about the nature of faith for a minute. The dictionary definition of the word is "complete trust or confidence in someone or something,"[2] but an even simpler one-word definition might be "reliance." To have faith is, at its root, to rely on something we believe to be reliable. Now if that's true, then by definition, faith can have no virtuous quality in itself. It cannot stand alone; in fact, it comes into being only when it leans on or relies on something else. It is, considered in itself, fundamentally empty.

Maybe it will help us understand this concept if we use a metaphor. Faith is like a hand; it grasps other things as it trusts and relies on them, whether those things are people or bank accounts or superstitions or even Christ. When we have faith in something, we are reaching out and taking hold of it in trust. What follows from that, though, is that faith, like a hand, is empty until it takes hold of something else. The fact is, there's nothing inherently good or bad, virtuous or blameworthy in simply grasping; whether the grasping is good or bad depends entirely on what is grasped. If you're stumbling, it's good to grasp a handrail but it's not good to grasp a hot stove! Well, in the same way, there's also nothing inherently good or bad in simply trusting; it depends entirely on the object of our trust. So, here's the fundamental reality: faith is empty of goodness or badness until it takes hold of something else.

This is a profound point to grasp if you struggle with assurance. In my pastoral experience, many Christians' struggles with assurance are rooted in a fear that their faith is not strong enough, or big enough, or pure enough—that it's simply not *good* enough to meet whatever standard God has set for "acceptable" faith. But that's just the point. There's no such thing as a good or acceptable faith, only a good or acceptable *object* of faith. The value of your faith isn't in the faith itself; it's in *what that faith is trusting*. Here's the point: The worry that unsettles so many Christians—"Is my faith good enough, strong enough, and pure enough to meet God's standard?"—is entirely the wrong question. The right questions are rather "What is my faith *in*? What am I trusting, hoping in, and relying on to secure my access into God's presence, and is *that* good enough, strong enough, and pure enough to meet God's standard?" And if your answer to those questions is "My faith is in Christ," then the answer to the question whether he's good and strong and pure enough is a universe-shaking *yes*! "This is my beloved Son," God said, "with whom I am well pleased!" (Matt. 3:17).

But isn't it true that faith *can* be stronger or weaker? Can't we trust something to varying degrees? Well, yes, of course. But throughout the Gospels, Jesus also seems to be at pains to make it clear to his disciples that the relative strength or weakness of their faith is *not* finally what determines if that faith is acceptable or saving. Look, for example, at this famous passage from Luke 17:

> The apostles said to the Lord, "Increase our faith!" And the Lord said, "If you had faith like a grain of mustard seed, you could say to this mulberry tree, 'Be uprooted and planted in the sea,' and it would obey you." (vv. 5–6)

When we read passages like this, we often get distracted by the striking image of a man uprooting a tree with a word—as if faith somehow works like an X-Men superpower. But the uprooted tree isn't the point here; that's hyperbole. The point is Jesus's teaching about the size or strength of faith. And do you see the force of his answer? The disciples want bigger, stronger faith, but he tells them essentially that the size and strength of faith aren't what's important at all; it's the *existence* of faith. Even faith as small as a mustard seed (proverbially the smallest of all seeds) is enough to uproot trees or move mountains. Even in Matthew 17:20, when Jesus tells his disciples they are men of little faith and that faith like a mustard seed can move mountains, his point is not that their faith is only the size of, say, an orchid seed and now they need to work hard to grow it to the size of a mustard seed. His point is, at this time in their lives they are really men of *no* faith, and if they had faith in him even the size of a mustard seed their faith would be effective.

There's one more encouraging reality to see here about the nature of faith. By its very definition, faith includes some measure of assurance. It simply has to, because it is, after all, reliance, and relying on something requires that you have some certainty that it is reliable. If you walk out onto a bridge across a ravine, then by definition you must have at least some confidence and assurance that the bridge isn't going to collapse. Otherwise you wouldn't walk out there in the first place. In the same way, if you have faith in Christ, if you're relying on him to save you, then you must have at least some confidence and assurance that he will in fact save you. Otherwise you wouldn't trust in him or call on his name at all. Paul made this very point in Romans 4. Abraham's faith, by definition, meant that he was "fully convinced that God was able to do what he had promised" (v. 21).

So, why does all this matter when it comes to assurance? It matters for at least two crucial reasons. First, it gives us a reason to stop obsessing over whether our faith is good enough to meet God's standard of an "acceptable" faith. That's the wrong question entirely. The right question is not "Is my faith acceptable?" but rather "Is the object of my faith acceptable?" One of those questions will focus your mind and heart on yourself, and the other will focus them on Jesus. Second, it reminds us that assurance is not fundamentally something separate from faith, something that you get later if you're really lucky or really good. No, some degree of assurance is present in faith right from the beginning. You wouldn't trust Jesus if you weren't, to some degree at least, confident and assured that he is trustworthy. So, do you have faith in Jesus? Do you trust him? Then the fundamental reality is that you do think he is trustworthy. You do have confidence—to some degree or another—that he will keep his promise to save sinners or you wouldn't trust him in the first place. That confidence may not be very strong right now, and it may not be big, and it may even be mixed and mingled with all kinds of doubt and fear, but it's there. And that's a really good, and really comforting, mustard seed–sized start.

I hope you can see now why I've said that the gospel of Jesus Christ is the first source of Christian assurance. Because at every step it calls us to recognize our own spiritual bankruptcy and to put our trust in Jesus, who irrevocably secures our access to God's presence. As long as we're trying to prove that we're acceptable to God by making ourselves less sinful, making ourselves more worthy of what Christ did for us, or making sure our faith is up to some acceptable standard of size or strength, our assurance will collapse as fast as we can build it. Why? Because we'll never be anything less than catastrophically sinful. Because we'll never be remotely worthy of Christ's love and work. And because our faith has no inherent value anyway, especially if what we're fundamentally trusting and relying on is self.

But if we hear the call of the gospel, recognize our own helpless sinfulness, and trust in Christ's promise to save hopeless sinners, assurance will begin to take root—not in the sand of our own struggle to be acceptable, but in the rock of his own infinite trustworthiness and value.

The Driving Sources of Assurance

The Promises of God

I f the gospel of Christ is one of the sources and drivers—the "accelerators," if you will—of our assurance, another is the promises of God. Sadly, promises don't hold much cachet these days. We don't trust them, and in fact the phrase "I promise" can cause as much skepticism as confidence. Between mendacious politicians, unfaithful spouses, and underhanded companies offering "guarantees" and "warranties" with more fine print than bold print, we just don't trust promises much anymore.

Because of that general atmosphere of mistrust, many of us find it difficult to embrace even *God's* promises as a source and driver of assurance. Of course, most of us probably don't doubt him immediately. We don't say, "I just don't believe you, God. I think you're a shyster, and you're trying to pull one over on me." We tend to have at least a little more respect than to doubt him so straightforwardly. Still, though, in the back of our minds, there's often a nagging fear we'll do something that will cause God to reconsider. Or even if we know God will technically keep his promises, we're still afraid we'll find out at the end that there was some fine print in them we didn't read carefully enough or some qualification we didn't quite meet. "Sorry, Greg," says Peter at the gate, "but apparently you didn't read paragraph 347, subsection B, which *clearly* states that no less than an average of *four* quiet times per week shall be necessary to prove the saving quality of your faith!" Let's be honest: some of the fears that lurk in the back of our minds can end up sounding way too much like a *Far Side* comic!

For all our general distrust of promises, though, the fact remains that the Bible presents God's promises, which are solid and irrevocable, as a powerful source and driver of assurance. It encourages us to trust them, to rely on them, and to continually *deepen* our understanding of and confidence in them. Think about how Paul described Abraham's faith in Romans 4. Abraham became "fully convinced that God was able to do what he had promised" (v. 21), and as he did so, "he grew strong in his faith" (v. 20). Do you see the logic there? Abraham's increasing conviction of the solidity of God's promise resulted in a strong faith and sense of assurance.

The same logic shows up again in Hebrews 10:23: "Let us hold fast the confession of our hope without wavering, for he who promised is faithful." What's the exhortation in that verse? To "hold fast the confession of our hope without wavering," which is another way of saying we should have assurance of our inheritance with Christ. But look carefully at the second half of that verse. Do you see what the author says is the source of that holding fast without wavering? It's that "he who promised is faithful." Again, the logic is clear: the more we become convinced God *will* keep his promises, the stronger our faith and assurance will be. For the author of Hebrews, it is axiomatic that our faith and therefore our assurance are driven and fueled by our considering the promises of God—and by extension, also the character of the God who makes the promises.

Don't miss the point in all of this: our sense of assurance and confidence depends on the strength of our trust in God to keep his promises. If we doubt God's determination to do what he has said, then we can be sure that our sense of assurance and confidence will waver. But the more we understand the simplicity and beauty of the promises God has made, and the more we understand how *unthinkable* it would be for him to break those promises, the stronger and more solid our confidence will be.

The Promises that Ground Our Assurance

In the most expansive sense, it would take an entire book to catalogue and revel in all the promises God has made throughout the course of history. There are promises of salvation and redemption, promises of a Messiah-King and a Suffering Servant, promises of deliverance for God's people and the destruction of God's enemies, promises of a new heaven and a new earth, and promises of a world where there is no sun because the light of God himself illuminates the universe. In that sense, the entire Bible is a book of divine promises, some already kept and others still awaiting their fulfillment. For our purposes of thinking about assurance, though, two categories of promise are particularly important: first, God's promise to save everyone who comes to Jesus Christ in faith; and second, God's promise to make sure none of those who come to him are finally lost. With those two promises, the divine Word secures both the beginning and the end of salvation. So, let's look at them a little more closely to see how they can encourage us toward confidence in God.

The New Testament is chock-full of this first promise, that God will save everyone who comes to Christ in faith. This is not simply a hope that Christians have, as if it's our best guess as to what God might want from us. Rather, God has declared to all heaven and earth that there is a way of salvation, and it is to trust in his Son, Jesus Christ. Jesus himself makes that promise in perhaps the most famous verse in the entire Bible, John 3:16: "For God so loved the world, that he gave his only Son, that whoever believes in him should not perish but have eternal life." Then just two verses later, he addresses the matter again just as clearly: "Whoever believes in him is not condemned" (v. 18). Later in the book of John, Jesus attributes this promise of salvation directly to his Father: "For this is the will of my Father, that everyone who looks on the Son and believes in him should have eternal life" (John 6:40). And again, "Truly, truly, I say to you, whoever believes has eternal life" (v. 47). Paul also declares God's promise to save those who come to Jesus in faith. For example, look at Romans 10:9: "If you confess with your mouth that Jesus is Lord and believe in your heart that God raised him from the dead, you will be saved." And verse

13 of the same chapter: "Everyone who calls on the name of the Lord will be saved."

Promises like these are everywhere in the New Testament. In fact, just as one example of many, take a look at all the places where the New Testament uses the phrase "everyone who believes." What you'll find is nothing less than a treasure chest of promises from God!

- "To him all the prophets bear witness that *everyone who believes* in him receives forgiveness of sins through his name." (Acts 10:43, emphasis added)
- "By him *everyone who believes* is freed from everything from which you could not be freed by the law of Moses." (Acts 13:39, emphasis added)
- "I am not ashamed of the gospel, for it is the power of God for salvation to *everyone who believes*, to the Jew first and also to the Greek." (Rom. 1:16, emphasis added)
- "Christ is the end of the law for righteousness to *everyone who believes*." (Rom. 10:4, emphasis added)
- "For the Scripture says, '*Everyone who believes* in him will not be put to shame.'" (Rom. 10:11, emphasis added)
- "*Everyone who believes* that Jesus is the Christ has been born of God." (1 John 5:1, emphasis added)

Now, let's pause here for a moment, because if you're like me, your heart is probably already looking for the fine print. "Sure, all right," we say, "but what exactly do you mean by *believe*? Is my believing strong enough? Is it big enough and pure enough? The devil, you know, is in the details." Listen, I understand entirely the temptation to think like that;

those thoughts threaten to flood my mind too when I hear the promises of God. But if those are your first thoughts, you might want to read the last section of chapter 2 again, because that kind of thinking may very well betray a heart that's trying to turn faith into an inherently valuable *contribution* to your salvation rather than the empty hand that simply grasps the gift that God offers.

Besides, why is the first move of our hearts always to think God is trying to catch us in the fine print? I mean, think about the people whom Jesus embraced. Most of them were not exactly paragons of a flawless, grade-A faith in him. Their faith was broken and imperfect and sometimes even mixed with doubt. Take, for example, the woman with the issue of blood, whose faith rose only so far as to make her try to *sneak* a healing from Jesus before he could notice. He told her that her faith had made her whole (see Mark 5:25–34). There was also the man in Mark 9 who pleaded with him in desperation, "If you can do anything, have compassion on us and help us" (v. 22), which drew an incredulous response from Jesus: "'If you can'! All things are possible for one who believes" (v. 23). Even then, the best faith the man could muster was a muddy jumble of belief and doubt, and he knew it: "I believe; help my unbelief!" he cried (v. 24). Then there was the thief on the cross, whose faith was late and unadorned and unproved and even contrary to the entire tenor of his life to that point, and yet Jesus said to him, "Truly, I say to you, today you will be with me in paradise" (Luke 23:43).

Do you see the point of all this? In due course, yes, we will consider the difference between a dead faith and a living one, a false faith and a true one. That's a real and important distinction. But when God promises he will save those who believe in Jesus, no insidious fine print defines faith so narrowly that only the best, most spiritual people will ever be able to pluck it like pure gold from the heights of Olympus. Jesus says, "Come to me, all who labor and are heavy laden, and I will give you rest" (Matt. 11:28), not "Come to me, you who are heavy burdened and holding up marvelously under the weight!" As we've already seen, faith is by its very nature a recognition of one's own spiritual bankruptcy, an admission that we need saving. It's a mark not of spiritual valor but of spiritual surrender. And God's inviolable promise is that those who come to his Son—weary, broken, and with imperfect faith—will be saved.

A second category of promise also bears directly on our assurance. Not only does God promise that he will save all those who come to Jesus, but he also promises throughout the New Testament that none of those who do so will be lost. In John 6:37–40, for example, Jesus says again and again that those who come to him will not be lost but will be raised up at the last day.

> All that the Father gives me will come to me, and whoever comes to me I will never cast out. For I have come down from heaven, not to do my own will but the will of him who sent me. And this is the will of him who sent me, that I should lose nothing of all that he has given me, but raise it up on the last day. For this is the will of my Father, that everyone who looks on the Son and believes in him should have eternal life, and I will raise him up on the last day.

Jesus not only promises that he will never cast out one who comes to him in faith but also says that it's his Father's will that he should lose not a single one of those believers but rather raise them all up at the last day. Later, in John 10:27–30, he explains *why* he won't fail to raise them up:

> My sheep hear my voice, and I know them, and they follow me. I give them eternal life, and they will never perish, and no one will snatch them out of my hand. My Father, who has given them to me, is greater than all, and no one is able to snatch them out of the Father's hand. I and the Father are one.

Why will they never perish? Because they are held fast in his strong hand—and also in his Father's strong hand!—and therefore no one will ever be able to snatch them away. What an incredibly encouraging promise this is, that Father, Son, and Spirit (as we'll see in the next chapter)—the entire Triune Godhead—are united in their determination to bring us safely home. If you'll let that truth reach its full force in your heart, it will have a powerful tendency to settle your doubts and calm your fears. As the hymn says,

> He will hold me fast!
> He will hold me fast!
> For my Savior loves me so;
> He will hold me fast![1]

There are other promises in this vein as well. Paul writes this in Philippians 1:6 regarding the believers there: "I am sure of this, that he who began a good work in you will bring it to completion at the day of Jesus Christ." Peter too speaks of believers in 1 Peter 1:5 as those "who by God's power are being guarded through faith for a salvation ready to be revealed in the last time." What a precious truth that must have been to Peter in particular! You have to wonder if he remembered Jesus's words to him on the night of his denial: "Simon, Simon, behold, Satan demanded to have you, that he might sift you like wheat, but I have prayed for you that your faith may not fail. And when you have turned again, strengthen your brothers" (Luke 22:31–32). How deeply and personally Peter must have rejoiced at the thought of God guarding him—even through his own catastrophic sin—and holding him fast until the last day!

Perhaps most of all, there's Paul's "Golden Chain of Salvation" in Romans 8:29–30:

> For those whom he foreknew he also predestined to be conformed to the image of his Son, in order that he might be the firstborn among many brothers. And those whom he predestined he also called, and those whom he called he also justified, and those whom he justified he also glorified.

Do you see the gloriously relentless logic of this promise? It might be clearest if you start at the end and move backward. Who finally gets glorified? It's those who are justified. And how many of those who are justified finally wind up being glorified? One hundred percent! From justification to glorification, there is no loss whatsoever. Everyone who is justified is finally glorified. Now, notice that the 100 percent logic runs all the way back to the beginning, even to eternity-past when God foreknew—which is to say, foreloved—his elect. Paul's promise here is as watertight as Jesus's own, rooted in eternity-past and stretching into eternity-future. If you come to Christ in faith, you *will* be glorified and raised up at the last day.

Do you see? God promises that everyone who comes to Christ in faith will be saved *and* that all those who come to Christ in faith will be preserved until the end. Those are strong promises, to be sure. But doubt rises again when we begin to think, *Well, sure. But we all know those promises will be revoked if we don't prove ourselves worthy of them!* And then, once again, the hopeless, miserable slog toward self-assurance by works begins. Don't let that happen! The truth is, from start to finish, the Bible is at pains to show us that God is determined to keep his promises to his people. This is true even when a person looks for all the world like they deserve to have his promises revoked, even when they have given him every reason imaginable to say, "You know what? Never mind." Once again, the message is this: You'll never make yourself worthy of what God has done for you. Your only hope is to rest and find assurance in his promises.

A famous but obscure story in the Old Testament makes this point in a striking and even humorous way. It's the story of King Balak and the sorcerer Balaam. Most people know the story simply as "The Story of the Talking Donkey," but there's far more to it than that. Some background first. The story is told in Numbers 22. After forty years of wandering in the wilderness and the death of an entire generation, the people of Israel had finally come a second time to the edge of the promised land, and the question was whether this time they would be able to enter and take the territory God had given them. Meanwhile, one pagan king of the region named Balak realized the Israelites had become a threat to him, and so since he couldn't match them militarily, he decided to hire a famous sorcerer named Balaam to wrestle God into cursing his people instead of blessing them. From there, the hijinks began, because Balaam desperately wanted the money King Balak had offered him, but try as he might with all his tricks of sorcery, he simply couldn't wrestle God to the ground. In fact, every time he tried to curse the people, God forced him to bless them instead, at one point even thwarting Balaam's plans by having his donkey rebuke him!

But here's the hidden hook in the story. As Balaam stands on the mountain and looks down over the people of Israel, the reader is supposed to know that these are the people of a broken, failed nation. Why? Because even though the sinful generation had died in the wilderness, the *new* generation was just as sinful; they rebelled against God in exactly the same way their parents had. To make matters worse, Aaron the high priest was now dead. And to cap off the catastrophe, even the great Moses had disqualified himself from the promised land when he took out his frustrations on God by striking the rock instead of speaking to it as God had commanded. From top to bottom, then, Israel was a wrecked people, and it wasn't illegitimate to wonder at this point if God might revoke his promises altogether this time. The people would have deserved it, in spades.

And yet . . . from the top of the mountain rang out God's blessings over them—a reiteration of all the promises he had made—and this time from the lips of a pagan sorcerer who really didn't even want to speak those blessings in the first place! The nation below had spiritually collapsed; they had rebelled against God, forfeiting any claim they might have had to his promises. And even Moses—the one who had been charged for decades with speaking God's promises to the people—was off the scene in disgrace. And yet still God found a way. Even in the midst of the collapse, God still found a way to reaffirm his promises and blessings to his people. You see the point God is fairly screaming at us through this story? So unbreakable are his promises, so unalterable are his blessings, that even if God has to use a reluctant pagan sorcerer and a talking donkey to reaffirm them yet again, he will.

That's massively encouraging and comforting, isn't it? God finds a way to pronounce these blessings over a broken people. And why is it so encouraging? Because you and I are broken people! If God's promises were solid only for those who have it together, who are unfailingly faithful, who are courageously and powerfully proving themselves to be worthy of those promises all the time, we'd be in a hopeless situation. But that's not how God's promises of grace work. He says to the weary and heavy laden, not the pure and victorious, "Come to me, and I will give you rest."

The Reasons for God's Unfailing Determination to Keep His Promises

There's another question we need to ask at this point, and it's one that drives the solidity of God's promises even deeper. Here it is: *Why* is God so determined to keep his promises, especially his promise to save and preserve all those who come to Christ by faith? In other words, why can't he simply say, "Never mind" at some point? What grounds God's determination to keep those promises? The answer to that question takes us into some deep theological waters and provides us with even more reason to rest on God's promises.

The first reason God is determined to keep his promises is rooted in his own divine character. Simply put, it would be flatly incompatible with his very nature—indeed, with his very identity—for God to break or revoke his promises. God says this about himself in the Bible many times. For example, Paul in Titus 1:2 simply affirms that "God . . . never lies." Even Balaam himself says this in Numbers 23:19: "God is not man, that he should lie, or a son of man, that he should change his mind. Has he said, and will he not do it? Or has he spoken, and will he not fulfill it?" And the author of Hebrews even ties this truth about God's character directly to our assurance: "By two unchangeable things, in which it is impossible for God to lie, we who have fled for refuge might have strong encouragement to hold fast to the hope set before us" (6:18). What he means by "two unchangeable things" is that God has both *promised* and *sworn* that he will save and preserve those who trust in Jesus, and it is therefore unthinkable that he would fail to do so.

There's a second reason that God is determined to keep his promises: his unbreakable devotion to his Son and his commitment to glorify and honor him. In fact, the New Testament makes it clear that the whole point of God's plan of redemption was to glorify Christ. Just before Jesus went to the cross, he prayed, "Father, the hour has come; glorify your Son that the Son may glorify you" (John 17:1). In Philippians 2:9–11, Paul reveals the ultimate goal of the plan of redemption:

> Therefore God has highly exalted him and bestowed on him
> the name that is above every name, so that at the name of
> Jesus every knee should bow, in heaven and on earth and

under the earth, and every tongue confess that Jesus Christ is Lord, to the glory of God the Father.

Even the angels in the book of Revelation worship the Son because of his work of redemption:

> Worthy are you to take the scroll
>   and to open its seals,
> for you were slain, and by your blood you ransomed
>   people for God
>   from every tribe and language and people and
>   nation,
> and you have made them a kingdom and priests to
>   our God,
>   and they shall reign on the earth. (5:9–11)

Do you see why God's commitment to his Son's glory so powerfully grounds the confidence we can have in God's promises? If God were to revoke his promises, he wouldn't be revoking only his promises to *you*. He would be revoking his promises to *his Son*. If he failed somehow to keep his promise to preserve believers until the end and raise them up at the last day, he wouldn't just be failing believers; he would be failing Jesus. *And that will never happen!* You see? If you are a believer in Christ—united to him by faith—then your salvation is not ultimately grounded in your waffling, wavering commitment to him. It's grounded in God's eternal, unbreakable determination to honor his Son *by saving you*. That's why not one of those the Father has given to him will be lost.

The promises of God are a powerful driver of assurance, once you understand them and begin to let your heart rest in them. God has promised that he will save all those who come to Christ in faith *and* that not one of those who comes to him will be lost. What's more, God's determination to keep his promises is grounded in his own eternal character and in his unbreakable determination to glorify and honor his Son, our Savior. Dear friend, learn to trust those promises. Deepen your understanding of them, of God's character, and of God's love for his Son, and you'll find yourself resting more and more comfortably in the full assurance of faith.

The Supernatural Source
of Assurance

The Witness of the Spirit

The summer after I turned forty years old, I decided more or less on a whim to take a two-week trek to Mount Everest Base Camp. My wife and kids insist it was a midlife crisis. I say it was an adventure, not to mention proof of my continuing youth and vitality! However you want to look at it, though, it was an amazing trip, full of utterly exotic experiences and breathtaking vistas I doubt I will ever see again.

Our hikes every day began very early in the morning. I never quite figured out why, but I think it was at least in part to make sure there would be enough daylight to react if anything ever went wrong. At any rate, most mornings we were at breakfast by 6:00 a.m. and hitting the trail by 6:30. Then, often by noon, we'd arrive at the day's goal—a

Nepalese teahouse where we'd eat, sit in the common room, read or talk to other trekkers, eat again, and then go to bed around 9:00 p.m. Sometimes the afternoon would involve an acclimatization hike during which we'd climb a nearby ridge, ascending a thousand or so feet, and then descend again to sleep.

Honestly, the hikes could be frustrating sometimes, not so much because of the difficulty but because of the clouds. There were entire afternoons when the clouds were so thick we couldn't see anything farther than the nearest ridge. Imagine knowing that the snowcapped Himalayas are *right there* in front of you and yet not being able to see them. That was the situation on one of our acclimatization hikes, which I'd been told would be one of the most beautiful hikes of the trek. We were supposed to ascend to a peak called Nangkar Tshang; it was the first time we would cross 16,000 feet (5,000 meters) in altitude, and the views of a mountain called Ama Dablam were said to be breathtaking. So, off we went, and for two hours we saw nothing but clouds. Occasionally, we would think the air was clearing, only to realize another bank of clouds was rolling in.

When we reached the peak of Nangkar Tshang, I took a picture of my altimeter reading because there was nothing else to take a picture of! Then we headed down. I kept squinting my eyes, knowing Ama Dablam was there, but I was unable to catch the slightest glimpse of it. Then, in one unbelievable instant, it happened. Over just a few seconds, the clouds dissipated, and there it was—what some people say is the most beautiful mountain in the world towering over me closer and larger than I ever imagined. I'm not easily brought to tears, but the beauty and enormity of that mountain—the sun all of a sudden glinting off its white faces—did it, and I found myself singing a hymn to the Creator. There was just enough time to snap a few pictures before, just as suddenly, another cloud bank moved in and Ama Dablam vanished. But it was there. I knew it was there, even if it was invisible to me now. But, oh, what an amazing thing it was to be able to see it—not just to know it was there in an objective but blind way but for it to be clearly and gloriously visible to my own eyes!

That kind of experience, in part, is what we mean by the witness of the Spirit. At times in this journey, we may know with all objective confidence that the truths of the gospel and the promises of God are there and true, and yet not be fully sensible of them; we may not see and experience them. But sometimes the Holy Spirit parts the clouds and gives us a vision of those promises in all their enormity that simply takes our breath away.

The Bible's Teaching on the Spirit's Witness

The phrase "witness of the Spirit" comes from Romans 8:14–17, where Paul uses it to describe how the Holy Spirit cries out with our own spirits that we are in fact children of God:

> For all who are led by the Spirit of God are sons of God. For you did not receive the spirit of slavery to fall back into fear, but you have received the Spirit of adoption as sons, by whom we cry, "Abba! Father!" The Spirit himself bears witness with our spirit that we are children of God, and if children, then heirs—heirs of God and fellow heirs with Christ, provided we suffer with him in order that we may also be glorified with him.

He uses the same idea in Galatians 4:4–7:

> But when the fullness of time had come, God sent forth his Son, born of woman, born under the law, to redeem those who were under the law, so that we might receive adoption as sons. And because you are sons, God has sent the Spirit of his Son into our hearts, crying, "Abba! Father!" So you are no longer a slave, but a son, and if a son, then an heir through God.

There are several important points to note here. First, notice that in both of these passages, the witness of the Spirit—that is, the Spirit crying out with our spirits that we are children of God—is closely connected to the fact that God has *adopted* us as his children. What an incredible truth! Not only have we been forgiven, justified, and regenerated, and not only has God promised that he will one day glorify and enthrone us on high with Christ, but God has also actually made us his sons and daughters. This is therefore no distant, cold, clinical, transactional salvation. God has brought us into the closest imaginable relationship with him—beloved, accepted, and welcomed sons and daughters of the King. That's the context in which Paul teaches that the Spirit witnesses to us: he reminds us, and the universe itself, that even when we struggle, even as we trudge through the acrid smoke of the battlefield, we are children of God.

Notice too that the one who cries, "Abba! Father!" in each passage is different. In Romans, it is the believer—you, me—who cries out, while in the Galatians passage, it is the Spirit himself who does so. These two passages taken together create one of the most beautiful images in the entire

Bible. In the Romans 8 passage, the situation seems to be one of near desperation. "You did not receive the spirit of slavery," Paul writes, "to fall back into fear" (v. 15). In other words, Paul doesn't envision believers as having a leisurely stroll through the park here. They're in danger and hard-pressed—tempted in fact to sink through fear and back into the dark slavery of sin. They're on their knees in the smoke of battle, yet even through choked lungs they still cry out, "Abba! Father!" I've had experiences like that. Maybe you have too. And in those moments of desperation, my "cry" is more like a whisper, sometimes choked with tears. "Abba . . . Father . . ."

But then think about Galatians 4:6, which says, "Because you are sons, God has sent the Spirit of his Son into our hearts, crying, 'Abba! Father!'" The believer may whisper, but at that precise moment, the Spirit streaks out of heaven like a lightning bolt, joining his voice with the weak, desperate cry of the Christian and splitting the heavens like thunder: "Abba! Father! This is a child of God!" he cries, even when all we can muster is a choked whisper.

It's critically important to see in all this that the witness of the Spirit—and the assurance it brings—is not a special gift that God gives to some Christians and not others. Some theologians have understood it that way, but that doesn't seem to be the teaching of the Bible. On the contrary, the Bible couldn't be clearer that the Spirit is given to every believer, not sometime later in life but at the very moment of salvation. In fact, the Old Testament taught, and Peter reaffirmed in his sermon at Pentecost, that the pouring out of the Spirit was one of the primary marks of the dawning of the messianic age. In other words, if you don't have the Spirit, you're outside the Messiah's kingdom. To be a child of the King is to have his Spirit dwelling in you. Paul teaches this when he speaks of the Holy Spirit as a "seal" in Ephesians 1:13–14:

> In him you also, when you heard the word of truth, the gospel of your salvation, and believed in him, were sealed with the promised Holy Spirit, who is the guarantee of our inheritance until we acquire possession of it, to the praise of his glory.

Do you notice what Paul says about *when* a person receives the seal of the Spirit? It's not sometime after salvation but "when you heard the word of truth . . . and believed in him." The Spirit's coming into your life and beginning his work of testifying with your spirit that you are a child of God happened the moment you bowed your knee to Jesus and trusted in him for salvation.

Notice also that the Spirit's presence and witness are guarantees of our future, final salvation. When he cries out that we are children of God, that doesn't mean "just for now" or "but we'll see what happens." The indwelling presence of the Spirit in our lives is a down payment on our future salvation, or as Paul put it, "The guarantee of our inheritance until we acquire possession of it" (Eph. 1:14). His cry reverberates through the eons right to the foot of the throne, right to the moment when we are fully and finally declared righteous in God's sight because of Jesus.[1]

There's another important issue to consider here, though, because the Spirit's witness in our lives is not always equally sensible to every believer at every moment. Yes, it is always there; as long as the Spirit lives within us, he bears witness with us that we are children of God. But his witness will be more obvious to us at certain times than at others. Paul seems to acknowledge this when he writes in Romans 5:

> Not only that, but we rejoice in our sufferings, knowing that suffering produces endurance, and endurance produces character, and character produces hope, and hope does not put us to shame, because God's love has been poured into our hearts through the Holy Spirit who has been given to us. (vv. 3–5)

Paul certainly seems to be talking here again about the witness of the Spirit—his role of pouring into our hearts God's love and making us sensible of it. But look when that happens: just like in Romans 8, he ties the witness of the Spirit to hard, dark times, times when suffering produces endurance, character, and hope. So, it seems that it may be especially in the hard times, even more than in the easy ones, that the Spirit cries out with a little more volume and parts the clouds so that we become sensible of God's love for us even more than usual.

The Spirit's Witness and Our Assurance

In light of everything we've learned here, we must keep in mind a few important points regarding the Spirit's witness. First, we should always remember to keep this third source of assurance—the supernatural witness of the Spirit—in perspective. The witness of the Spirit is not meant to be the primary driving source of your confidence that you are a Christian. If you want your assurance to grow and strengthen, the solution is not simply to sit quietly and hope the Spirit will do it. The solution is to give yourself to deepening your understanding and embrace of the gospel and God's promises. That in itself will strengthen your faith and assurance, but here's the thing: it will also give the Spirit the material he *always* uses to settle and assure your heart.

Think about Paul's statement again in Romans 5:5, that "God's love has been poured into our hearts through the Holy Spirit who has been given to us." This verse is referring to a personal, direct experience of the love of God given by the Spirit. But that Spirit-mediated experience of God's love doesn't happen out of the blue, as if it were some mystical, trancelike state. How do we know that? Because Paul tells us in the following verses *how* the Spirit pours the love of God into our hearts. Here's what he says:

> For while we were still weak, at the right time Christ died for the ungodly. For one will scarcely die for a righteous person—though perhaps for a good person one would dare even to die—but God shows his love for us in that while we were still sinners, Christ died for us. (vv. 6–8)

The word *for* there at the beginning is important. It signals that the Spirit pours the love of God into our hearts *because* these things are true. In other words, the Spirit's witness is not content-less. When he pours the love of God into our hearts, he actually takes these very truths of the gospel and makes them sensible to us, igniting them in our hearts. Here's the point: If you want a heightened experience of the Spirit's witness (which is there all the time to some degree and has been since the moment you became a Christian), don't perform some Eastern meditative practice of emptying your mind and waiting on some ecstatic experience. Rather, ask God to give you that experience, but then do the work of stacking your heart with the doctrinal fuel the Holy Spirit ignites. Again, the point is, even when it comes to the witness of the Spirit, the fountainheads of our assurance are the gospel of Jesus Christ and the promises of God. Those are the very things the Spirit uses to pour out an experience of the love of God into our hearts.

Also critical to remember in this regard is that assurance of salvation doesn't consist solely of the Spirit's witness, and even less does assurance consist of our *experience* of the Spirit's witness. We've already said that every believer has the Spirit dwelling within them, and therefore the Spirit does his witnessing work in every believer's heart. But he doesn't do so in the same way and with the same intensity at every moment. There are times in life when the Spirit's direct witness seems relatively quiet to us, sometimes even imperceptible. But that doesn't mean it is absent, and it also doesn't mean we should despair of our salvation during those times. On the contrary, our response when the witness of the Spirit seems quiet ought to be to drive our hearts ever more purposefully to the gospel and God's promises, praying that the Lord will help us have more confidence in them and that the Spirit soon ignites them in a sensible experience of God's love.

Here's another important point. It's critical to keep in mind also that the witness of the Spirit does not trump the other sources of assurance. It always comes in harmony with the other three. Now, on one level, that's an obvious point to make. If we're not believers in Christ, then there will be no witness of the Spirit in our hearts because the Holy Spirit will not dwell in our hearts at all. But in a less obvious sense, the witness of the Spirit also cannot be used to negate the testimony of the fourth, confirming source of assurance—the fruits of obedience, which we'll consider in a later chapter. Here's what I mean: if our lives are marked not by obedience to Christ but rather by unrepentant sin and allegiance to the world, then we can't simply say something like, "Well, those things don't matter because I feel the witness of the Spirit in my heart." Listen to what Paul says in 1 Corinthians 4:4–5:

> I am not aware of anything against myself, but I am not thereby acquitted. It is the Lord who judges me. Therefore do not pronounce judgment before the time, before the Lord comes, who will bring to light the things now hidden in darkness and will disclose the purposes of the heart. Then each one will receive his commendation from God.

Paul's point here has more to do with his own conscience than with the witness of the Spirit, but the idea is the same. Just because our conscience is clear or we *think* the Spirit is witnessing with our spirits does not mean everything is fine. If our lives are characterized by darkness, we should not take comfort in a feeling.

Conversely, though, sometimes a believer's experience of assurance is weaker than perhaps one would expect. That's when the witness of the Spirit becomes more precious than gold. Here's how B. B. Warfield puts it:

> A man who has none of the marks of a Christian is not entitled to believe himself to be a Christian; only those who

are being led by the Spirit of God are children of God. But a man who has all the marks of being a Christian may fall short of his privilege of assurance. It is to such that the witness of the Spirit is superadded, not to take the place of the evidence of "signs," but to enhance their effect and raise it to a higher plane; not to produce an irrational, unjustified conviction, but to produce a higher and more stable conviction than he would be, all unaided, able to draw; not to supply the lack of evidence, but secure a disease of the mind which will not profit fully by the evidence. . . . The function of the witness of the Spirit of God is, therefore, to give to our halting conclusions the weight of his Divine certitude.[2]

Finally, we have to ask if there's anything we can do to make it more likely that the Spirit will witness in our souls in this way. Probably the most important answer to give to that question is "Yes, trust in Christ for salvation!" After all, that's when the Spirit begins to dwell in us, and it's when he begins to testify with our spirits that we are children of God. Still, though, is there anything we can do to experience an unusually *strong* witness of the Spirit, a direct and immediate sense of comfort and rest in our salvation? Well, yes, there is. We can pray for it. That's exactly what Paul does for the Ephesians in Ephesians 3:14–19. He asks the Lord to help them know and experience "what is the breadth and length and height and depth . . . [of] the love of Christ that surpasses knowledge" (vv. 18–19). And who makes Christ's love sensible to us in that way? Who "pours into our hearts" the love of God? It's the Holy Spirit (see Rom. 5:5). Paul is praying that the Ephesians would strongly experience the witness of the Spirit, and it is right and good that we should do the same—both for ourselves and for others.

It's also important to remember here that the Bible seems to indicate that the Spirit tends to give an unusually strong witness not as a kind of spiritual "surprise party" but as wartime reinforcement in the midst of particular hardship, when our own voices have fallen weak and what we need most is encouragement to endure. Maybe that's in the midst of suffering; maybe it's in the fires of temptation. But it's when we have come to the end of our ability to cry out with our own voice, that the Spirit is most likely to thunder forth with *his* in testimony that we are children of God.

When it comes to the witness of the Spirit, probably the best thing we can do is not to try to manipulate or buy or find it in any way but to pray that God would make the love of Christ sensible and visible to us and then make sure we're stocking our minds with gospel truths and divine promises so the Spirit can ignite those truths in our hearts when he chooses to do so. After all, like Paul says in Romans 5, the Spirit's witness isn't just an untethered *feeling*; it consists in the Spirit pouring the love of God into our hearts, putting the truths of the gospel in front of our eyes, and supernaturally clearing away the clouds so we can see them in all their sunlit beauty.

The Undermining of Assurance

The Lies We Believe

A few years ago, I was walking through a particular area of downtown Louisville when I noticed a series of thunderous *booms* crashing through the city's air every few seconds. No one around me seemed too concerned, but it was a little disconcerting. My mind cycled through the possibilities. Was it thunder? No, too rhythmic. Automobile accidents? No—since when do wrecks happen every few seconds in a regular pattern? Bombs dropping? Possible . . . but unlikely.

I didn't solve the mystery until a few days later when I was driving on the interstate that runs along the Ohio River. Construction had just begun some weeks earlier on a massive new bridge across the river, and now as I looked out across the water I saw what was producing those thunderous booms. Floating on the water was an enormous barge with a towering structure rising from its deck. Every few seconds, some sort of engineering marvel inside that structure would hammer down with enormous force on what I assume was a steel beam, driving it deeper and deeper into the riverbed below. Eventually, that beam would make its way through the unstable mud and silt at the bottom of the river and bite, finally, into bedrock. And the deeper into that bedrock it was driven by the powerful machine above it, the stronger the bridge's foundation would be.

The memory of those steel beams being driven into bedrock has stuck with me over the years because it's a wonderful image of what it means to build a foundation for Christian assurance. The currents of life will always flow around and push against us, but as long as our confidence is driven deep into the bedrock of the gospel of Jesus Christ and the promises of God, we'll be able to stand firm in the full assurance of faith. To be sure, that's not easy work. Just as it took repeated, ear-splittingly powerful hammer blows to drive those steel beams into the riverbed, so it takes concerted and repeated effort to make sure our confidence and assurance are grounded in the gospel and the promises rather than in ourselves and our own efforts. That's been our work so far—to identify spiritual bedrock and begin to drive our confidence deeply into it. Even while we were yet sinners, Christ died for us, and God himself has *promised* that everyone who believes in him *will* have eternal life.

At this point, though, we should take some time to see and guard against another threat to our assurance. Imagine for a moment if some enemy decided to take down Louisville's new bridge across the Ohio River. They could use several strategies to do so. If they wanted to take it out quickly, a few well-placed explosives could do the trick in an instant. But what if they wanted to do it more slowly, maybe even make the whole thing look a bit more like a natural process? One idea would be to invent some way to gradually intro- duce a powerful acid into the bedrock that would soften it and eventually make it too weak to support the bridge's foundation. The process would be slower than explosives, but just as effective. Given enough time, the whole bridge would come down.

When it comes to our assurance, there are times when life and the Enemy himself set off explosives under our as- surance. But it seems that far more often one of Satan's greatest strategies for destroying our assurance is to in- troduce a cocktail of acids into the very bedrock of our understanding of both the gospel and God's promises to those who trust in Jesus. And what are those acids? Lies. Untruths that make the gospel seem less trustworthy and the promises of God less reliable and less comforting. And once those satanic lies have done their work, our assurance collapses into the water.

In this chapter, we'll spend some time looking at four of those assurance-dissolving lies and think together about precisely why they are untrue and how we can defend against them. Be careful not to let yourself off the hook too easily here. Sometimes, yes, we can embrace these lies as conscious theological principles. But the sad and dangerous truth is that sometimes we find ourselves believing lies without even really being conscious of doing so, and these "hidden" lies can be the hardest to identify and root out. As we consider these four lies, then, ask yourself not just whether you'd consciously affirm them as positive theological principles but also whether they might sometimes sneak into your hidden assumptions without you even really noticing.

Lie #1: Jesus Loves Me, but God the Father Really Doesn't

Theologically and historically speaking, this lie—Jesus loves me, but God doesn't—has had a long and notorious history, usually taking the form of drawing a hard distinction between the God of the Old Testament and the incarnate God of the New Testament. The heretic Marcion once declared that the God of the Old Testament was an evil and wrathful deity whom Jesus had come to oppose and defeat. Marcion even began his New Testament at Luke 4:31—"And Jesus came down to Capernaum . . ."—as if Jesus simply descended from heaven!

Not many people consciously believe that anymore, of course, but the idea that God the Son and God the Father are somehow at odds with each other when it comes to our salvation still shows up subtly now and again. You may even have heard this falsehood in gospel presentations or sermons. "Jesus stood between you and the Father's wrath," the preacher will say. "When God the Father, the Great Judge of all the earth, would have destroyed you for your sin, Jesus spread his arms on the cross and cried, 'No!'" Of course, it's true that Jesus *did* in fact exhaust the Father's righteous wrath against sin when he died on the cross. He was without doubt, as Paul says in Romans 3:25, "a propitiation," a sacrifice of atonement that satisfies and exhausts God's wrath. It's also true that those who persist in rebellion against God will endure not only the metaphorical "wrath" of sin's natural consequences but also the personal wrath of God the

Father, the all-righteous Judge of all the earth. "Whoever believes in the Son has eternal life," John writes, but "whoever does not obey the Son shall not see life, but the *wrath of God* remains on him" (John 3:36, emphasis added).

But to think of God the Father as a wrathful Judge and God the Son as the One who stands in his way and absorbs his anger is fatally simplistic. It's not true, and it doesn't even begin to capture what the Bible teaches about the love of the Triune God. Take the propitiation language from Romans 3, for example. Who offered Jesus as a propitiation? *God the Father* did. And Christ's death for us while we were still sinners is precisely how "God shows his love for us" (Rom. 5:8). Don't miss the logical progression here. It's not that Jesus died for us while we were sinners and *then* God loved us. It's that God loved us and *therefore* Christ died for us while we were sinners. Look also at what Paul writes in Ephesians 2:

> You were dead in the trespasses and sins . . . and were by nature children of wrath, like the rest of mankind. But God, being rich in mercy, because of the great love with which he loved us, even when we were dead in our trespasses, made us alive together with Christ—by grace you have been saved— and raised us up with him and seated us with him in the heavenly places in Christ Jesus, so that in the coming ages he might show the immeasurable riches of his grace in kindness toward us in Christ Jesus. (vv. 1, 3–7)

Who saw us in our sin-induced calamity and acted to save us? It was God! Just as God the Son died for us while we were still sinners, so God the Father set the wheels of redemption in motion while we were dead in trespasses and sins. And look at the reason he did so. It was "because of the great love with which he loved us," a love that erupted from his own divine character, which is "rich in mercy." But that's not even the end. Look at the *goal* God has for showing this love to sinners. It's so that in the coming ages—that is, for all eternity—he might pour out on them "the immeasurable riches of his grace in kindness toward us in Christ Jesus."

This is a powerful truth when it comes to the strength of our assurance. If we believe the lie that Jesus loves us but the Father simply *tolerates* us because Jesus insists on it, then we'll always harbor a fear that God doesn't really want us in his presence. He will seem distant, fearsome, and forever faultfinding, and the result will be a nagging desire to *escape* him rather than run to him. The theologian John Owen writes pointedly about how this lie undermines our assurance:

> How few of the saints are experimentally acquainted with this privilege of holding immediate communion with the Father in love! With what anxious, doubtful thoughts do they look upon Him! What fears, what questionings are there, of his good will and kindness! At the best, many think that there is no sweetness at all in God towards us, but what is purchased at the high price of the blood of Jesus.[1]

Of course, it's true that the blood of Jesus is the means by which God's love comes to us and benefits us. "That alone is the way of communication," Owen says. But then he puts the truth beautifully: "But the free fountain and spring of all is in the bosom of the Father (1 John 1:2)."[2] Owen is exactly right. Your salvation is not an act of Jesus *in opposition* to his Father but rather in perfect union with his Father and the Spirit. If you are a believer, then you can be assured that the entire Triune Godhead—God the Father, God the Son, and God the Holy Spirit—is united in love and power to save you and bring you safely home.

So, don't for a moment believe the devil's lie that Jesus loves you, but the Father doesn't. Don't be afraid that God the Father is holding his nose as Jesus brings you into his presence, or looking away in disgust and barely managing to hold back his wrath, or even that he only began to love you once Jesus died. On the contrary, remember that salvation sprang like a fountain from his own eternal riches of mercy and love, and revel in the fact that God rejoices over you even now with singing, celebrating that his wayward child is back in his arms.

Lie #2: God Is Fundamentally Stingy and Naturally against Us

As Genesis 3 records, Satan convinced Adam and Eve to join him in his rebellion against the Most High God by blatantly lying to them. As flagrant as his lie was, though, it was also insidiously subtle, leading Adam and Eve to doubt not just one or two things God had *said* but also, and even more importantly, who God *was*. Essentially, Satan's lie came in two parts from his forked tongue. First, he simply and flatly contradicted God's promise from Genesis 2:17 that Adam and Eve would surely die if they ate from the tree in the center of the garden. "You will not surely die," Satan said (Gen. 3:4). With that, he tempted Eve to doubt God's word.

The second part of his falsehood, though, was arguably even more evil, for it tempted Eve to doubt not just God's word but his *character.* "For God knows that when you eat of it your eyes will be opened, and you will be like God, knowing good and evil" (v. 5). Satan wanted Adam and Eve to believe that God was denying them something good and desirable, revealing himself to be fundamentally stingy, ungenerous, and unloving. Of course, nothing could have been further from the truth. God had placed Adam and Eve in a beautiful garden full of trees that would meet their every need and fill them with every joy. He had even *commanded* them to enjoy the fruit of those trees, but Satan's triumph was to close Adam's and Eve's eyes to God's boundless generosity and focus their minds on the one thing in all creation God had withheld from them—a single tree, which was a reminder to them that their freedom and authority were limited by his own. What the serpent injected into Adam's and Eve's minds that day was a venom that convinced them God was not generous and loving and *for* them but rather fundamentally crabbed and stingy and selfishly *against* them.

One pastor, Sinclair Ferguson, evocatively calls this satanic falsehood "the Edenic poison," the lie of the "not-to-be-trusted-because-he-does-not-love-me false Father,"[3] and points out how this poison, once injected into the human psyche, spread universally and has affected sinful human beings ever since. This is how we think about God now; this is what we wrongly believe him to be—a God who desires *not* to give us joy and happiness but rather to withhold them, at least until we have paid enough to earn his grudging favor. And the sad truth is that this poisonous lie continues to affect us even after the powerful antidote of the gospel of free grace is administered. The gospel tells us that God is unspeakably loving and kind, that his favor does not have to be—indeed, *cannot be*—earned, but is offered as a free gift to those who believe. It tells us that salvation is not wrested from his unwilling hand but is lavished on his people for eternity out of the inexhaustible riches of his grace. That's what we believe when we embrace the gospel—and yet still we struggle not to succumb to the lie! The Edenic poison still numbs our minds, tempting us to think that God's blessings remain locked away—his heart closed, his face stern.

This is a critical point when it comes to our assurance of salvation. When assurance weakens and dies, this is always the rot that has infected the root of faith—a suspicion that the gospel is not really free, that redemption is not really a gift, that what Jesus really meant when he cried out, "It is finished" was "I've done my part; now it's your turn to do yours." And so we begin to wonder whether our lives truly merit what God is offering, and we assume he is looking down at us, wondering the same thing. And the result of that, as we look into our hearts and see the sin and selfishness that still boil there, is doubt and fear and shame before the eyes of a God we imagine to be shaking his head in disgust.

But how different is the truth of the gospel from that venomous lie. According to Ferguson, the gospel is like a specially designed antidote to the Edenic poison.

> The gospel is *designed* to deliver us from this lie. For it reveals that behind and manifested in the coming of Christ and his death for us is the love of a Father who gives us everything he has: first his Son to die for us and then his Spirit to live within us.[4]

Dear Christian, does this Edenic poison still course through your veins? Then drink deeply of the antidote of the gospel. Remember the infinite well of love from which your salvation springs, the fathomless generosity of a Father who would deliver his only Son to death for your sake, and the bottomless riches he has promised you in eternity (Rom. 8:32). Satan is a liar. The Lord is not stingy and ungenerous and *against us*. He is Immanuel, God with us, God *for us*.

Lie #3: Jesus Is Merely the Means to the Greater End of Heaven's Blessings

Mansions in glory. I remember, as a child growing up in a Baptist church in Texas, mentally measuring the drapes (and the tennis court!) for the mansion waiting for me on the shore of the Crystal Sea. "I've got a mansion just over the hilltop," we'd sing in church. "We will never more wander, but walk on streets that are purest gold!"[5] *All praise to Jesus*, I thought, *for getting me such a good deal!*

Eventually, I matured as a Christian and realized that the mansion and the gold pavement aren't really the point—God is. Being in his presence, seeing his face. But even once we get past the point of thinking about eternity in terms of the real estate, we Christians still have a natural tendency to think of the blessings of salvation as abstracted from (that is, separate from) Jesus. So the thinking goes that Jesus, because of what he did for us, has the right and ability now to give us the blessings of eternity—eternal life, glorification, heaven, the new heaven and new earth, all of it. He has access to it, we think, and can give it to us if he decides to do so. In the end, though, he is merely the means by which we obtain the greater end of heaven's blessings.

Of course, the Bible teaches no such thing. Jesus is the Alpha and the Omega, the beginning *and* the end, and the greatest blessing of heaven is not mansions or streets, even ones made of gold, but rather to behold the King there in his beauty, to see him face-to-face, and to be in fellowship with him forever. To most Christians, that's not a new thought; we know deep down that the Giver matters far more than the gifts he gives, and that he himself is the right object of our affections. But a subtle variation on this theme often creeps into our thinking and can be surprisingly toxic to a strong sense of assurance and confidence in Christ. What is that error? It is to abstract and separate salvation itself from Jesus—not in the sense of thinking that salvation can be attained without him (it can't) but to think of salvation as something distinct from him and after him, something he *can* give if we come to him in faith, but that we have not yet grasped even if we have grasped him.

Here's how the acid of this lie works: When we think of Jesus as the *means* of salvation—rather than the very *essence* of it—our minds immediately begin to ask the question "How do I get salvation?" instead of "How do I get Christ?" And the result will always be that our hearts will begin striving to convince the One who can give salvation that we are worthy of it and that he should in fact give it to us. But as we've seen time and again, that kind of thinking will sink us into a vortex of trying to attain self-assurance, a project that is doomed to fail and thus will always prove to be depressingly futile.

But the wonder of the gospel is that salvation is not something separate from and distinct from and after Christ. To have Christ is to have salvation. "Christ Jesus," Paul writes, "became to us wisdom from God, righteousness and sanctification and redemption" (1 Cor. 1:30). See the point there? Jesus does not merely *give* those things; he *is* those things. To have him is to have them.

Here's the thing: If salvation and its blessings are distinct from Christ, and he is merely a means to the end of obtaining them, then no real rest can be found in him. Rest can only be had at some point *after* him. But if we take the Bible to heart in understanding that to embrace him is to embrace salvation, then we can rest in the knowledge that our salvation really is finished; once we have embraced him, there is nothing greater, nothing more beautiful, nothing after or beyond, and we can rest in the full assurance that by having him, we have all.

The Philippian jailer asked Paul and Silas, "Sirs, what must I do to be saved?" (Acts 16:30). In all likelihood, he wasn't expecting the answer they gave him. Probably he was thinking they would tell him, right in line with his question, some things to do. Maybe he would have to help them escape from prison, or perform some sacrifices, or convert to Judaism. Who knows? The point is, he was frightened by what God had done around him that night, and he wanted to know what God required of him now. Paul's answer was likely not at all what he was anticipating because it didn't call on him to do *anything* except to embrace in faith the One who had already done everything. "Believe in the Lord Jesus, and you will be saved" (v. 31). It wasn't, "Believe in Jesus, then do these things, and you will be saved." It was simply, "Embrace Jesus, and in so doing, you embrace salvation."

If the question in our minds is "How can I obtain salvation?" then the answers to that question will ramify into a thousand demands on our time and attention. The requirements will overwhelm us. Instead, we must embrace the answer the Bible gives. How can I obtain salvation? *By obtaining Christ.* And how do I obtain Christ? Simply and solely and only by faith.

If you have embraced Christ by faith, dear Christian, there is nothing else—nothing else to be done to win salvation and nothing greater to be obtained. By embracing Christ, you have embraced righteousness and salvation. Rest in that truth, and revel in the fact that all that is lacking is the moment when you will look finally into the face of your Redeemer, your Salvation, your King. The great blessing of salvation is not a mansion you do not yet have. It is Jesus himself, and you *do* have him—right here and right now.

Lie #4: God Has Opened a Door of Salvation, but He Is Largely Indifferent Regarding Who Walks Through It

So many of the lies we believe are variations on the second one we considered—the Edenic poison that God is fundamentally stingy and against us—and this one is no different. Lie number four is the thought that while God has opened the door of salvation and invited us to come in, he largely stands now as an uninterested doorman, welcoming those who come but not uniquely invested in the salvation of any particular person. In a way, this error rises from a misunderstanding of biblical verses such as 1 Timothy 2:4, which says God "desires all people to be saved," and 2 Peter 3:9, with its teaching that God is patient with us, "not wishing that any should perish, but that all should reach repentance."

Understood rightly, these verses are a wonderful affirmation of God's Creator-love for all human beings. He made us all, and therefore as our Creator, he loves us. But verses like these also do not tell the whole story of God's love, and if we imagine they do, we will fail to appreciate God's passion for his people. We'll picture him as offering a generalized invitation to salvation for all humanity but then stepping aside and disinterestedly allowing those who will to accept it. But the Bible actually says far more about God's love than that. In fact, the Bible talks about several kinds of love that God has for his creation and his people.

The deepest and most profound divine love the Bible teaches is the love that lies at the essence of God's very character and nature, the mutual love shared eternally between Father, Son, and Holy Spirit in the unity of the Godhead. "God is love," John says (1 John 4:8), and therefore the love he shows for us is nothing less than the overflow of his own eternal nature.

Even in its overflow, however, that eternal, divine love takes several forms. First, there's the general love that God has for his entire creation, including the nonhuman parts of it. This is reflected in his declaration in Genesis 1:31 that "God saw everything that he had made, and behold, it was very good." Jesus too tells of how God's Creator-love shows itself in his care for the birds of the air and even the grasses of the field (see Matt. 6:25–30). Second, though, there is also the particular love God has for all humanity, that is, for all those who are created in his image. This is a higher love than creation-love, a love reflected in verses such as 1 Timothy 2:4 and 2 Peter 3:9, which highlight that God's basic desire for all humanity is that none should perish.

But our understanding of God's love can't stop there, because the Bible teaches another aspect of God's love that is not general but rather is focused on individuals. We've already seen this particular love in Ephesians 2:4–5, in which Paul writes that "God, being rich in mercy, because of the great love with which he loved us, even when we were dead in our trespasses, made us alive together with Christ." Do you see the unique nature of that "great love with which he loved us"? That's not just a general love for all humanity, and we know that because the *result* of it is that God makes us alive in Christ. If that "great love" were generalized to include all humanity, then all humanity would be made alive in Christ. No, this is a particular, individual, distinguishing, *electing* love.

Another passage in which we see this particular electing love of God is Romans 8:29–30, right at the beginning of what is often called "The Golden Chain of Salvation." At the fountainhead of that chain is Paul's affirmation that "those whom he foreknew he also predestined." Some misunderstand the word *foreknew* as simply a kind of divine foresight into the future, as if God looked down through history, saw those who would respond to him in faith, and predestined those who met that qualification. But the Bible knows nothing of that kind of divine fortune-telling in regard to salvation, and as so often is true in the Bible, the word *knew* is not just about bare knowledge but *intimacy*. The word means that God "fore*loved*." And what happens to those who are foreloved by God in this way? They are—all of them—predestined and then called and then justified and then glorified. To be so foreloved by God in eternity-past is to be assured of being glorified in eternity-future. Again, this is a specific, personal, discriminating love.

Do you see the importance of this concept to our sense of assurance? It lies here: our confidence that we will finally be saved depends largely on how sure we are that God actually loves us. So, if my vision of God is that he is largely indifferent to me as an individual—that he's glad for people to come through the doors of heaven but doesn't much care *who* they are—then I will always be tempted in a thousand ways to doubt whether he really cares if I am there with him in the end or not. And that in turn will introduce distance and coldness and suspicion into my relationship with him. The Edenic poison will flow again through my heart.

What the Bible teaches, though, is the exact opposite of that. God's love for us is personal and individual and specific and passionate. If our faith is in Jesus, if we are clinging to him, then God has had his love set on us since before the foundation of the world. The Son of God knew us *by name* and his response to our slavery under sin, to our death in our transgressions, was not a ho-hum stroll to the doors of heaven and a bored "Come if you want" invitation. No, his response was to roar from his throne with the shout, "I'm going to get them!"

Dear Christian, you are loved—specifically, individually, and particularly. Never for a moment believe the lie that God is somehow indifferent as to whether you finally make it safely home. On the contrary, he has given all the resources of divine omnipotence to the cause of bringing you to his embrace. Why? Because the number of the elect, the population of heaven—the very mission of his Son—would be incomplete without you. Revel again in these words, because they are about *you*:

My sheep hear my voice, and I know them, and they follow me. I give them eternal life, and they will never perish, and no one will snatch them out of my hand. My Father, who has given them to me, is greater than all, and no one is able to snatch them out of the Father's hand. I and the Father are one. (John 10:27–30)

One in essence, one in glory, and one in omnipotent determination to raise you up at the last day!

Looking Ahead

So far in this book we've considered three of what the Bible holds out as sources of our assurance. We've seen how the gospel of Jesus Christ undermines at every step our own tendency to desire *self*-assurance and throws us helpless on the person and work of Jesus Christ. But we've also seen how despairing of our own self-worth and learning to trust and rely on Christ alone for our salvation provide an immovably secure foundation for our confidence and assurance. He is the same yesterday, today, and forever; he has finished the work of redemption; and therefore, as the old confession puts it, "he is a compassionate, a suitable, and an all-sufficient Savior."

We've also considered how God's promises to save all those who come to Christ in faith and to preserve them until the end provide another solid foundation for our assurance. If God has promised something, then he *must* do it or else violate and contradict his own character. Therefore, if he has said he will save those who come to Christ in faith, he will save those who come to Christ. If he has said he will lose none of those who come but raise them up at the last day, then he will lose none of those who come. In fact, to fail or default on either of those promises would be not just to contradict his own character but also to impugn the honor of his Son.

Those two immovable truths—the gospel of Jesus Christ and the promises of God—are the sources, the drivers, the accelerators of our assurance. If you want to increase your assurance and confidence and faith, focus there. Put the weight of your attention and energy there. Study and meditate on the gospel; remember and deepen your understanding of God's promises, as well as his own character and love for his Son that undergird them. Assurance is never strengthened by trying to make yourself more worthy of salvation, much less wallowing in worry and guilt that you're *not*. God does not call you to make yourself worthy of the blessings of eternity; he calls you to recognize and trust in the fact that Christ is worthy on your behalf and in your place.

Finally, we've seen how the Holy Spirit, who dwells in us as a guarantee of our future inheritance from the moment we trust in Christ, testifies with our own spirit that we are children of God. Especially in the times when we are hard-pressed by temptation and hardship, he parts the clouds so that we can see the gospel of Jesus Christ and the promises of God in all their glorious beauty.

There's still more to consider, though, because the Bible holds out one more truth that bears on our assurance. It's not a *driver* of assurance, but it is an indicator that we are children of God, and therefore it also bears on our sense of assurance. That indicator is the fruit of good works. It's to that topic that we now turn.

The Confirming Source of Assurance

The Fruits of Obedience

Besides the gospel of Jesus Christ, the promises of God, and the witness of the Holy Spirit, one more reality bears on the strength or weakness of our assurance— our own lives. My guess is that as a reader of a book like this one, you have been waiting for this chapter. Because despite all we've said so far about the other three sources of assurance, several nagging questions have been at the back of your mind: "How do I know my life doesn't show my faith in the gospel to be a fraud?" "How do I know my works don't show my faith in God's promises to be false?" "How do I know my 'fruit count' doesn't prove that the witness of the Spirit in my heart is really *not* the witness of the Spirit at all?"

Those are important questions that plague many Christians who struggle with assurance of salvation. In fact, it's this source—the speedometer, so to speak—that shipwrecks assurance in countless Christians' lives.

Why is that? Perhaps the first answer we should give is that for some professing Christians, the speedometer reads "zero" because they really have no true faith. Their lives—shot through with sin and continuing, unrepentant rebellion against God—show that their faith really is empty. For such people, the fact that they have no assurance of salvation is not a bad thing at all. Their faith in Christ really is superficial and the speedometer is simply telling them so! Those people *shouldn't* have a strong sense of assurance of salvation because they truly have no genuine faith in Christ. For them, the solution isn't to *fix* the speedometer or to distrust it but rather to *listen* to it—to heed its warning, recognize that their "faith" is what James calls a "dead faith," and repent of their sin and trust in Jesus for salvation.

But sometimes and for some Christians—perhaps even for *most* Christians—that's not what's really happening when the speedometer wrecks their assurance. Rather, the problem is often that Christians simply don't understand how the Bible's teaching on good works functions theologically, and therefore they make mistakes in using it. In the next couple of chapters, our goal is thus to understand the speedometer—its purpose, function, and place in the architecture of assurance—and then to consider several ways Christians tend to misuse it.

Before we get started, though, it will be helpful to make two important observations about our good works and their role in our assurance. The first is that we're not spending so much time on this fourth source of assurance because it is the most important. We are spending the most time on it because it is the most complicated and therefore the most prone to being misunderstood and misused. It would be a crying shame if the result of having read this book was that your eyes became even more focused on yourself. Robert Murray McCheyne was exactly right when he counseled, "For every look at yourself, take ten looks at Christ!"[1] In the same way, I hope that after reading this book you understand the architecture of assurance better, and therefore I hope your eyes and heart are fixed more solidly on the gospel and the promises of God. Look at the fruit, yes. Let it be a warning to you when necessary and a confirmation when appropriate. But do not put your faith in it.

Here's the second observation: many Christians would be surprised to realize that when the Bible talks about the relationship between our good works and assurance, the purpose is almost always to *settle* believers' hearts and consciences, to *confirm* them and *comfort* them, not to terrify them. Here's an example. A few years ago, I announced to my church that I was planning to preach a short sermon series through the book of 1 John. I was astonished by the response to that announcement, because more than a handful of people communicated to me that they were terrified to hear those sermons. Why? Because they assumed the message of 1 John—with his three tests of genuine faith or marks of a true Christian— was meant to unsettle Christians' consciences, to make them doubt their salvation so that they'd be better behaved. In a certain sense, those people's fear of the message of 1 John was entirely legitimate; the book is notorious for making Christians doubt whether they really are Christians. In fact, nearly every time I've heard the book taught, that's exactly how it's been used—as a bludgeon to make Christians doubt.

But that's deeply ironic, and even wrong, because John repeatedly says his purpose for writing is so that his readers may *know* they are children of God, believers in Jesus, and heirs of eternal life. Look how that glorious word *know* echoes like a drumbeat throughout the book:

> By this we know that we have come to know him . . . Therefore we know . . . because you know . . . because you know . . . we know . . . you know . . . we know . . . you know . . . we know . . . we shall know that we are of the truth and reassure our heart before him . . . for he knows everything . . . we know that he abides in us . . . you know the Spirit of God . . . By this we know . . . By this we know . . . so we have come to know . . . By this we know . . . we know . . . we know . . . we know . . . we know . . . so that we may know . . . I write these things to you who believe in the name of the Son of God so that you may know that you have eternal life.

Thirty-seven times in thirty verses John says the goal of his book is knowledge, not doubt. Even as he lays out his three "tests" or "marks," their purpose is not ultimately to make Christians say, "Oh no, I'll never live up to that" but rather, "Okay, I can see those realities in myself, not perfectly, not completely, but they're there."

That's how most of the Bible passages that teach on these matters are supposed to function. Even the warning passages, such as Hebrews 6, for example, aren't there ultimately to terrify but rather to assure, even if that assurance comes by cautioning a believer to stay away from a deadly path. In this chapter, then, we'll begin to consider the Bible's teaching on how our own good works relate to our assurance.

How Good Works Are a Confirming Source of Assurance

Throughout history, some Christians have denied that our works should have any bearing on our sense of assurance at all. At some level, that's understandable, and for a few reasons. For one thing, there's always the danger that our focus will be too much on our works, even to the point that our faith subtly shifts from Christ to self. Thus, some Christians have argued that works can and should play no role in our assurance, but rather our entire focus should be on Christ and the gospel. Besides, those Christians have argued, until we stand with Jesus, our obedience will be so imperfect as to be a hopelessly unreliable indicator of the reality of our faith. In fact, the argument goes, to find any degree of confidence or assurance in our own works is antithetical to saving faith itself, which by definition requires a renunciation of confidence in our own works.

Those arguments hold some force, to be sure, and we always have to be careful to keep our faith firmly rooted in Christ, not ourselves. To fail in that would be more than unhealthy; it would be eternally deadly. But at the same time, it's also clear that the Bible draws a connection between the works we do and our sense of confidence that we really are Christians. Let's look at a few such passages.

1 John

One of the most obvious and famous parts of Scripture that draws a connection between our lives and our assurance is the entire book of 1 John. The book—which is really a circular letter—seems to have been written to a whole group of churches in a particular area, and John's purpose in writing it was to encourage and ground those believers in the faith, to strengthen them in their confidence in Jesus Christ and his work in their lives. The book's main feature is a set of three marks of a true Christian against which John encourages his readers to check themselves. And as they do, he says, they will grow in their knowledge that they have eternal life.

The first of those marks of a true Christian is a love for other believers. The connection between love and assurance is clear right from the very beginning of the discussion, when John says in 2:3, "By this we know that we have come to know him, if we keep his commandments." You might read that verse and wonder where it says anything about love, but look how John defines "his commandments" just a few verses later. He really couldn't make the point any clearer:

> Beloved, if our heart does not condemn us, we have confidence before God; and whatever we ask we receive from him, because we keep his commandments and do what pleases him. *And this is his commandment*, that we believe in the name of his Son Jesus Christ and love one another, just as he has commanded us. (3:21–23, emphasis added)

John identifies "his commandments" as two very specific things—to believe in the name of Jesus and to love one another. We'll talk about believing in Jesus in a moment, but do you see the logical connection here between assurance and loving others? We know we have come to know Christ, and we can have confidence before God *insofar as* we keep Christ's commandment, which is to love one another.

John's second mark of a true Christian is that they do not love the world, which some theologians have labeled the "moral test" of true faith. John first puts this point negatively in 2:15: "If anyone loves the world, the love of the Father is not in him." It's important to understand exactly what John means by "if anyone loves the world." It doesn't mean enjoying the gifts of God in this present age or even falling at times into sin (which, as John affirms clearly in 1:8, happens to every Christian). Rather, what John means by loving the world is a matter of a person's fundamental allegiance, the tilt of their heart. Here's what John is asking: What do you love? What gives you joy? What most powerfully entices your heart? What satisfies it? If you are in Christ, then the fundamental allegiance of your heart ought to reflect that. Your life should be marked by a love for the things of the light, not by a pining for the things of darkness. The logic is clear: if your life is marked by a fundamental allegiance to the darkness, then you have little ground for confidence that you are a child of light.

The third mark of a true Christian that John discusses is, unsurprisingly, that a person holds fast to the truth about Jesus:

> Who is the liar but he who denies that Jesus is the Christ? This is the antichrist, he who denies the Father and the Son. No one who denies the Son has the Father. Whoever confesses the Son has the Father also. Let what you heard from the beginning abide in you. If what you heard from the beginning abides in you, then you too will abide in the Son and in the Father. And this is the promise that he made to us—eternal life. (2:22–25)

This was the cardinal failing of those who had unsettled the faith of the Christians to whom John was writing this letter. They had abandoned the confession that Jesus was the Christ, left the fellowship of the church, and apparently begun preaching that salvation could be had in another way, probably through some strange and ironic combination of perfectionism (an assertion that they had no sin) and hedonism (loving the world and pursuing its pleasures). John's exhortation to the believers who remained, therefore, was to see that, unlike those who had left, they themselves still confessed Jesus to be the Christ, they were not living like children of darkness, and they maintained their love for one another. Therefore, they could have some confidence they truly were heirs of the promise of eternal life.

Galatians 5:16–24

The apostle Paul uses the same logic at the end of his letter to the Galatians. The entire letter, from the very beginning, is a biting polemic and devastating argument against any scheme of salvation by works. At the end, though, Paul exhorts his readers not to be given over to the works of the flesh but to be marked by the fruit of the Spirit. Paul creates a catalogue of works of the flesh: "sexual immorality, impurity, sensuality, idolatry, sorcery, enmity, strife, jealousy, fits of anger, rivalries, dissensions, divisions, envy, drunkenness, orgies, and things like these" and warns "that those who do such things will not inherit the kingdom of God" (vv. 19–21). It's important to note the tense of the verb *do*. The verse is not referring to those who *have done* such things but rather to those *doing* such things or, perhaps even more accurately, to those *who are doers* of such things. Just as in 1 John, the emphasis is not on the mere action but on the person's character. Paul is talking about people who claim Christ as Savior and yet whose lives are marked and characterized by these works of the flesh.

In contrast to these works of the flesh, Paul also lists nine virtues he calls "the fruit of the Spirit": "love, joy, peace, patience, kindness, goodness, faithfulness, gentleness, self-control" (vv. 22–23). These are the fruits that will increasingly mark a Christian's life.

Here's what to notice: even in the middle of this hot polemic against salvation by works, Paul isn't shy about turning his readers' attention to the fourth source of assurance. If a person's life was marked by gratifying the desires of the flesh, if it was characterized by these works of the flesh, then that person could have little confidence that the Spirit lived within them and therefore little assurance of salvation. But, of course, the reverse was also true. If Paul's readers could see in their lives the fruit of the Spirit—the evidence of his transforming work in them—then they could be confident that they would in fact inherit the kingdom of God.

Other Passages

This same logic turns up in other places in the New Testament too. James uses it in James 2:14–26 when he writes that a "faith" that does not result in good works is a *dead faith* (by which he means no faith at all), and the implication is that we can have some assurance of the genuineness of our faith if it *is* in fact producing a life of righteousness. Peter too talks about a life devoid of Christian fruit rendering us "ineffective and unproductive" in our knowledge of Jesus, while a life filled with fruit gives us confidence that we will receive a rich welcome into the eternal kingdom of our Lord and Savior Jesus Christ (see 2 Pet. 1:11). Paul, Peter, *and* James all say that even our sufferings produce a sense of assurance in our hearts because as we bear up under them, we see that our faith in Jesus is not superficial, but it is able to bear the weight of hardship, difficulty, and even persecution (see Rom. 5:3–5; 1 Pet. 1:6–8; James 1:2–4).

All this, of course, springs from Jesus's own teaching about a tree and its fruit:

> Beware of false prophets, who come to you in sheep's clothing but inwardly are ravenous wolves. You will recognize them by their fruits. Are grapes gathered from thornbushes, or figs from thistles? So, every healthy tree bears good fruit, but the diseased tree bears bad fruit. A healthy tree cannot bear bad fruit, nor can a diseased tree bear good fruit. Every tree that does not bear good fruit is cut down and thrown into the fire. Thus you will recognize them by their fruits. (Matt. 7:15–20)

Most immediately, Jesus is talking here about recognizing false prophets by their fruits, but the logic is the same as that used by later New Testament authors. A healthy tree bears good fruit; therefore, we can tell something about the health of the tree by considering the health of its fruit. If we see good fruit in our lives, we can have some degree of confidence that we have a healthy, vital faith in Jesus. But if all we see is bad fruit—or no fruit—that kind of assurance will be weak or nonexistent. The Bible clearly teaches that relationship.

Good Works Are Meant to Confirm, Not Terrify

Here's a question: Does the existence of this relationship between our lives and our assurance have to be terrifying? For many Christians, it is—and undeniably so. They know their lives could never measure up to God's standard, and so when they consider their lives and fruit, they conclude that their fruit is bad or insufficient, and they lose confidence that they're Christians at all. But that doesn't seem to be the way the biblical writers intended their words to be understood. In fact, the stated purpose of drawing the connection between works and assurance is usually not to create doubt at all but rather to bring assurance.

Take 1 John, for example. We've already noted that John's stated purpose throughout the book is to bring his readers to a deep confidence that they are heirs of eternal life. So many Christians, though, read John's letter and employ his tests in exactly the wrong way and therefore draw exactly the wrong conclusions. Understand his book rightly, though, and you'll see that he wants his readers to come away *more* assured that they are Christians, not less! So, where do we typically go wrong? Why does the book so often seem so frightening? Well, let me give you four practical guidelines for reading 1 John and applying its tests rightly and helpfully in your life.

First, keep in mind that the very *purpose* of John's tests was to bring clarity to his readers. John wrote precisely to cut through the fog that a group of false Christians had created and to give believers some clear, imminently answerable questions they could ask themselves. One of the most striking things about John's tests is that they are so simple and concrete and answerable. Do I affirm the truth about Jesus? (Yes!) Do I love other believers? (Yes!) Is my allegiance to the world? (No!) So often in our search for assurance, we tend to make up our own questions. Do I love God enough? Is it the right kind of love? Is my faith strong enough, my joy large enough, my passion hot enough? If those are the questions of assurance, then God help us, because none of them can be answered in a concrete and straightforward way. Here's the point: Don't make up your own questions. Use John's. They are simple, meaningful, and above all, straightforwardly answerable.

Second, keep in mind the *context* of John's tests. If you read his letter, you quickly come to realize that John had a definite idea of what failure of his tests looked like. In fact, he had in mind a whole group of people he thought had in fact failed—that is, these people who had been members of these churches but who had recently denied that Jesus was the Christ, had hated their fellow believers so much that they had abandoned the church, and had been so convinced they were in fellowship with God that they had felt perfect freedom to live immoral, wicked, hedonistic, world-loving lives. *That's* who John had in mind when he thought of someone failing his tests, and he wanted the believers to whom he was writing to be reassured in their faith, to realize much to their own joy, *Yeah, we're not like that.*

Third, keep in mind the *scope* of John's tests. He wanted his readers to look at and consider the whole picture of their lives, not just one brushstroke on the canvas. This is the point where many Christians go so catastrophically wrong, because they apply John's tests to one particular moment or area of their lives—usually the worst one—and then despair of their faith and salvation. We often read sentences like 3:6—"No one who abides in him keeps on sinning; no one who keeps on sinning has either seen him or known him"—and think, *Well, that's describing me, because day after day I keep on sinning, so there's no way I'm a genuine Christian!* But that's not at all how John intended these tests to be used. He knew Christians would commit sins, and he tells us the remedy for that is to confess those sins to our Advocate, Jesus (see 1:9). Rather, what he's talking about is a life characterized by rebellion against God. I think there are four main reasons for understanding him in this way, and not as pointing an assurance-destroying finger at one or two isolated sins.

First, notice that John writes repeatedly in his book that he's talking about someone who "keeps on sinning" (3:6) or "makes a practice of sinning" (3:4, 8, 9). That's more than just "to sin." It points to continual, deliberate, pervasive sin in a person's life.

Second, John describes this kind of pervasive sinning as "lawlessness," which is used in the Bible to describe not a single discrete breaking of the law but rather a heart's entire character (see 3:4). It's a deep-rooted, extensive, Satan-like rebellion against God and his Word.

Third, in the structure of John's book, this discussion of keeping on in sin is parallel to what is described in 2:15–17, in which John describes what he's talking about here as a love for, or allegiance to, the world. Here's the point: When John says someone who "keeps on sinning" cannot think they know Jesus, he doesn't want us to look at just one brushstroke of sin on the canvas of our lives. He wants us to look at the whole painting. It's not a question of whether the color of sin exists on our canvas; it does, and John knows it. It's a question of the dominant color.

Fourth, keep in mind the *goal* of John's tests, which is to encourage us to put our faith in Christ. He says as much near the end of the book:

> For everyone who has been born of God overcomes the world. And this is the victory that has overcome the world—our

faith. Who is it that overcomes the world except the one who believes that Jesus is the Son of God? . . . Whoever has the Son has life; whoever does not have the Son of God does not have life. (5:4–5, 12)

The worst mistake we can make with John's letter is to apply his tests and then think, with great self-assurance, *I have to fix the problem*, instead of running in empty-handed faith to Christ. And yet so many of us Christians do just that, when John would actually have his tests confirm our faith in Jesus, or—if they turn up a lack of love or a love for the world—send us running not to self but rather to our Advocate before the Father, Jesus the righteous. Thus, John's message is not "Here are some ways to make yourself morally worthy of the Father's love" but rather "If we confess our sins, he is faithful and just to forgive us our sins and to cleanse us from all unrighteousness" (1:9).

So, you see, read in its correct context, and with its ultimate purpose and goal in mind, John's little book is not necessarily terrifying. To be sure, some professing Christians may read his book and not see themselves reflected in it at all, but even then, the right response is not to cower in terror but to repent and believe. But John's aim was not to terrify his original readers. It was to settle them, to calm them, to encourage them, and it is meant to do the same thing for most of us too. If we hold fast the truth about Jesus, if we have a genuine love for other believers, and if the dominant character of our lives is allegiance to Christ and not the world, here's what John says: "I write these things to you who believe in the name of the Son of God, that you may know that you have eternal life" (5:13).

Conclusion

Let's take stock of what we've said so far about this fourth source of assurance. Beginning with Jesus's own teaching about a tree and its fruit, and continuing in several places throughout the New Testament, the Bible teaches that our lives and fruit *do* in fact stand in relationship to our sense of confidence that we really are Christians. For most Christians, as for the original readers of 1 John, that reality is not supposed to create a sense of terror but a confirmation that the Spirit really is at work in us producing the fruits of righteousness. For some, though, it will serve as an urgent warning, as it should have for the false Christians in 1 John who had denied the truth about Jesus, abandoned the church, and embraced allegiance to the world.

For all its usefulness, though, it's critical to remember that this fourth source of assurance is *confirming*, not *driving*. In other words, it would be a terrible mistake to think that the way to increase our confidence and assurance is simply to do things to make our lives better. We are to look at the fruit of the Spirit in our lives and be encouraged, but we are not to think, *I'll create more fruit and be even more encouraged!* The right way to increase assurance—as well as the fruit that then confirms assurance even more—is to put our focus on the gospel and the promises. If we get in the habit of staring at our own fruit in the hope of engendering a sense of assurance, we will be in serious danger of shifting our faith from Jesus to self. Therefore, focus on the gospel. Focus on the promises. And as you do, the fruits of salvation will grow, and in seeing them you will rejoice all the more.

Misusing a Good Tool

Mistakes We Make in Considering Our Good Works

O ver the years, my dad and I have embarked on a number of home improvement and home repair projects. We've taken down walls, built new ones, laid wood flooring and tile, painted, put down carpet, installed electrical wiring and plumbing, and finished a thousand other jobs. Usually, the job goes well. Sometimes it does not.

A few years ago, my dad and I decided to replace a door that led out to my backyard. As far as construction projects go, this one shouldn't have been too difficult. All we needed was the door, some hinges and screws, a doorknob assembly, and *voila!* New door. The only trouble was that the home improvement store didn't have the correct size door; they only had ones that were about six inches too tall to fit my home's opening. But then again, my dad is a master at this sort of thing, and he's proven it a hundred times over. "We'll just get the big door," he said, "and cut it off at the bottom so it fits." So that's what we did, and we were *so* careful about it. We bought a saw blade that would cut through metal and an end cap to cover up the jagged bottom of the door after it was cut. We measured twice, nay *three* times, to be sure nothing would go wrong. Even the most obvious pitfall, the one you're probably expecting we fell into—the fact that if you cut the door off at the bottom, the doorknob won't fit where it's supposed to—we brilliantly anticipated and avoided. Instead of cutting *only* the bottom, we carefully made sure to keep the knob in the center by cutting six inches off *both* the top and the bottom, which, of course, adds up to twelve inches that we cut off the door.

It's a moment that's become Greg-and-Dennis legend in my family. For all our care, for all our having bought the best tools and having made the best, most careful measurements, we still did the job wrong. We misused the good tools we had, and the result was (hilarious) disaster.

Misusing good tools isn't always hilarious though. Sometimes it just leads to catastrophe. That's often the case when Christians try to analyze their own good works and fruit to increase their assurance. As we read in the last chapter, the Bible clearly teaches that examining our lives is a good tool, and it is a good thing to do; like a speedometer on a car, it can tell us if things are running smoothly or if something's wrong. And we can find ourselves being either encouraged even more in the faith or warned that our focus has somehow gone awry. But as with any good tool, there are so many wrong ways to use it, to do that analysis in a way that it was never meant to be done. And when Christians make those mistakes, the results can be catastrophic to assurance.

In this chapter, then, our goal is to consider some of the mistakes we tend to make when we start to do the work of examining our own fruit. My aim here is not to convince you that you *shouldn't* practice self-examination; it's simply to lay down some guardrails that might help you avoid doing that work wrongly. It's true that Paul commands us to examine ourselves (see 2 Cor. 13:5), but that doesn't mean we should do so however we see fit. There are ways to do it well and ways not to do it well.

The Practical Syllogism and How to Use It

At some point, Christians realized the Bible's teaching about good works and their relationship to salvation and therefore assurance is actually a bit of classical logical reasoning known as a *syllogism*. So, before we go on, let's talk a little formal logic. In a logical syllogism, a conclusion is drawn from two related premises that are asserted to be true. Here's a famous example:

All men are mortals.
Socrates is a man.
Therefore, Socrates is a mortal.

Sometimes, of course, a syllogism can be terribly wrong. An old cartoon once showed a penguin looking puzzled as he tried to use a syllogism:

Penguins are black and white.
Old television shows are black and white.
Therefore, penguins are old television shows.

And amusingly, here's *Google Dictionary*'s official example of a syllogism:

All dogs are animals.
All animals have four legs.
Therefore, all dogs have four legs.[1]

Wait a second . . .

Anyway, enough of the lesson in logic. The point is, Christians realized that the logical connection between good works and assurance—and the Bible's exhortation for believers to examine themselves and draw a conclusion from what they see—is in fact a "practical syllogism" (the word *practical* points to the fact that this syllogism has to do with our *praxis*, that is, our works) that runs something like this:

Good works are one characteristic of a true Christian.
I am characterized by good works.
Therefore, I have one characteristic of a true Christian.

We can even think about it in negative terms, like this:

If anyone loves the world, the love of the Father is not in him.
I love the world.
Therefore, the love of the Father is not in me.

Now, as long as we remember what John means by "love of the world"—that is, a fundamental allegiance to the world and its sinful patterns over against Jesus—then that's a perfectly legitimate logical conclusion. It's exactly the kind of reasoning other New Testament authors use in their books. And therefore, it's completely legitimate and good for us as Christians to do that kind of self-examination—to run this "practical syllogism" on our own lives and take the conclusion seriously.

That said, it's important to run that syllogism on our lives *correctly*, and that's where so many Christians go wrong and consequently find their assurance collapsing when it really should not be. So, let's consider six errors Christians often make in using this bit of Bible logic to examine their own lives.

First, it is a mistake to run the practical syllogism too narrowly.

Running the practical syllogism too narrowly is exactly the issue we mentioned in the last chapter regarding John's statement in 1 John 3:6 that "no one who abides in him keeps on sinning." John's intention is not that we should pick out one narrow point in our lives and, on the basis of staring at that, draw the conclusion that we are not really Christians. Rather, John intends for us to consider whether the whole tenor of our lives—the dominant color on our canvas—is allegiance to Christ or, as he calls it, "lawlessness."

This is a critical point because it is a mistake Christians make all the time when they begin to do the work of self-examination. By focusing too narrowly on one instance of sin or even on a single enduring struggle with sin—and then running the syllogism only on that narrow slice of their life—they wind up with a terrifically inaccurate assessment of

113

their true spiritual state. Think of it like this: on any given apple tree, even the most healthy one, we can always find one bad or rotten apple if we look carefully enough. Imagine taking a snapshot of that one bad apple, showing it to someone who hasn't looked at the whole tree, and asking them to make an assessment about the health of that apple tree based only on that one zoomed-in photo. The assessment would be suspect at best! And yet that's exactly what many Christians do with their own lives. They find the bad apple, the errant brushstroke on the canvas, and come to an assurance-crushing conclusion that they must not be a Christian after all.

The biblical and theological error in that kind of thinking should be obvious though. It draws on a wrongheaded perfectionism that fails to acknowledge the biblical teaching that even as Christians, we will still sin until the day we stand before Jesus in glory. The correct way to run the practical syllogism is not to run it on a single apple but to include in our field of view the whole tree—that is, to use a wide-angle lens instead of a zoom lens so that *all* the fruit is in view. In fact, the best way to examine ourselves may not be to use a photo at all but rather a movie, so we can take into account our growth in grace and holiness, our struggle against sin, and even our sorrow that sin still persists in us.

See? It's not the mere *presence* of sin in our lives that raises warning flags that we might not be a Christian. We shouldn't despair because we see a rotten apple on the tree, even one that hangs there for a long time. To be sure, if *most* of the apples are rotten or if the tree looks generally unhealthy, then that's a serious problem. We should never allow ourselves to become content or unconcerned about *any* bad fruit, as if it's no big deal if one branch of our tree is diseased or dead. We should always be seeking to identify, repent of, and eliminate *all* sin that shows up in our lives. But when it comes to our assurance of salvation, the Bible's exhortation to self-examination is intended to be obeyed broadly, with regard to the whole of our lives and not just one narrow slice of it. If we understand and apply that, we'll not only head off unwarranted, assurance-collapsing conclusions about ourselves but also be in a better position to see actual dangerous problems taking shape that demand action.

Second, it is a mistake to run the practical syllogism on a comparison of your life with others'.

The fact is, each and every Christian is on a unique path of sanctification and learning to follow Jesus. We all have different struggles, different victories, different hardships, and therefore to look at another Christian and reason, *I'm not as fruitful as she is, so therefore I must not be a Christian*, or *I struggle with this sin and he doesn't, so I'm probably not a Christian* is not a correct use of the syllogism.

And yet as nonsensical as it is, many Christians frequently use just that kind of reasoning. *If I don't have as much courage as Joni Eareckson Tada*, we think, *or as much passion as John Piper, or as much knowledge as Ravi Zacharias, or as much evangelistic zeal as Mack Stiles, then I can't possibly be a Christian.* Do you remember Trent from the beginning of this book? If you think about it, this was exactly the kind of reasoning that ultimately undermined and eroded his faith. He didn't see reflected in his own life the sparkling, sustained joy described in the book he was reading, and he wrongly concluded that he probably wasn't a Christian. His error wasn't in thinking that Christians are marked by joy. They are! Joy is one of the fruits of the Spirit; even in the midst of hardship and difficulty, Christians are marked by the joy of knowing that trials and tribulations will eventually pass and give way to eternity. No, Trent's mistake was in thinking that all Christians must experience joy in exactly the same way and to exactly the same degree. But they don't. For some Christians, the light of eternity shines bright in their eyes almost all the time. For others, the smoke of battle is so thick they can barely see eternity's light at all. Thus, it was a mistake—and a costly one—for Trent to compare himself to that one particular author, in one particular area, and conclude that he wasn't a Christian.

I doubt most Christians make this mistake in self-examination quite so blatantly as Trent made it. But even if it's less egregious, to base your assurance of faith on comparison with others is still wrongheaded. Of course, it's a good thing for Christians to have role models, examples to follow who are ahead of them on the journey. But that doesn't mean you should despair of your faith and conclude that you are not a child of God when you compare yourself to those role models. Think of it like this: My eight-year-old daughter is not as mature as my sixteen-year-old son. She is not as far along the road of growing up. But she is certainly no less my child because of that, and it would be wrong for her to conclude, *I'm not as far along in my growth and maturity as my brother, so therefore I am not as much my father's child as he is*. For my daughter to draw that kind of conclusion would be a terrible mistake—one that would leave her tragically, and falsely, doubting her father's love for her.

Third, it is a mistake to run the practical syllogism on the past instead of the present.

It's a great temptation for a Christian to consider the sins and patterns of their past and, on the basis of those, conclude that they could not possibly be a Christian. "How could a Christian have done the things I did?" they ask. But that's just the point of the gospel of Jesus Christ—it provides forgiveness for the past. Think about the apostle Paul. He persecuted the church of Christ to the point of trying to put believers in prison. Later, he would even call himself "the foremost" of sinners (1 Tim. 1:15). And yet Paul knew he had been forgiven of even that heinous sin. "I received mercy for this reason, that in me, as the foremost, Jesus Christ might display his perfect patience as an example to those who were to believe in him for eternal life" (v. 16). Paul knew his past sins were no match for Jesus's mercy, his past life no reason to think he was not one of God's children now.

The same is true for you, Christian. You may think back on your life and see a thousand sins for which God would have every right to condemn you. And the worst thing you could do is believe they are so bad that they make it impossible for you to be saved. As Paul discovered, God's mercy is an ocean of unfathomable depth, and even our greatest sins—once cast into it by Christ—are forever gone. In fact, that's exactly the point he seemed to be making to the Corinthian Christians:

> Or do you not know that the unrighteous will not inherit the kingdom of God? Do not be deceived: neither the sexually immoral, nor idolaters, nor adulterers, nor men who practice homosexuality, nor thieves, nor the greedy, nor drunkards,

nor revilers, nor swindlers will inherit the kingdom of God. And such were some of you. But you were washed, you were sanctified, you were justified in the name of the Lord Jesus Christ and by the Spirit of our God. (1 Cor. 6:9–11)

To be sure, there's the bracing warning that people characterized by unrighteousness will not inherit the kingdom of God. But Paul didn't mention those things with the intention of causing these believers to cower and think, *Oh no, that was me before I came to Christ; I must be unforgiveable!* On the contrary, he seems to bring up these old sins precisely to make the believers rejoice in the forgiveness they now have in Christ. Thus, he says, "Such *were* some of you" (emphasis added). Paul brought up these believers' past sins not to make them feel guilty, much less to doubt their salvation, but to encourage them to celebrate Christ's work and say, "Yes! I *was* that, but I am no longer because of Jesus!"

What this means is that the Bible intends for us to examine our *present* life, not our *past* one. The question is what our fruit looks like now, not what it looked like some time ago, much less before we came to Christ. Here's what the Bible says: Christ, through his work on our behalf, has set us free from both the condemnation and the guilt of past sin. If that's true, then there's no more tragic way to squander Christ's gift to us than to fasten the phantom chains of guilt on our wrists and allow them to rob us of the joyful assurance Jesus intends us to have. Examine your life, yes. But let your past sink into the ocean of God's forgiveness. Like the Corinthian Christians, you should not let your past be a source of fear and doubt; rather, think of it as a celebration for what Christ has done.

Fourth, it is a mistake to run the practical syllogism too frequently.

Though the Bible commands us as Christians to do the work of self-examination, it's entirely possible for a person to become obsessive in the practice, to the point that every individual word, thought, deed, and motivation becomes evidence—one way or the other—of the genuineness of the person's faith. That kind of introspective focus is unhealthy.

An analogy using fitness or wellness might be helpful. A person's weight may be an important and useful indicator of their overall health, but it would be entirely unhealthy for a person to weigh themselves a dozen times a day or after every meal. Not only would that show an unhealthy psychological obsession with what is finally only one of many indicators of health, but it would also fail to give an accurate or useful measure of the person's health at all. Even worse, the constant fluctuation—up and down, encouragement and discouragement—would likely leave the person incapable of taking the steps that would lead to true health. What's important is how a person's weight fluctuates over a few weeks, or even a few months, not a few minutes or hours.

In the same way, a tendency to spiritually "weigh" yourself using too frequent self-examination probably shows an unhealthy obsession with introspection—one that will cause enormous, perhaps even debilitating, fluctuation in your sense of assurance and also, ironically, prevent you from seeing your spiritual health clearly at all. Worst of all, a focus on frequent and unhealthy introspective examination will place you in danger of putting your hope in getting an A+ grade at any given moment rather than on Christ and his work.

Fifth, it is a mistake to do the work of self-examination alone.

When I was a child, some of the commercials that would air during Saturday morning cartoons would show children doing various dangerous stunts—jumping their bikes on ramps or turning flips on a trampoline. And at the bottom of the screen would flash the warning "Don't try this at home." In many ways, the work of self-examination should carry a similar warning: "Don't try this alone." The fact is, our hearts are inconceivably deceitful, which means we as human beings have a hard time seeing ourselves clearly and assessing ourselves rightly. Sometimes, perhaps most often, we tend to think too highly of ourselves and conclude that things are going well spiritually when actually they are not going well at all. Just as dangerously, though, sometimes we can be blind to the many good things the Holy Spirit is doing in and through our lives. The result is that we unduly focus on problem areas and therefore draw faulty conclusions about our actual overall spiritual health.

What this means is that we really should not make it a habit to do the serious work of self-examination alone. Sure, sometimes it's fine and good to take a look at our own lives, but it's even better—and safer—to examine ourselves with the help of other believers. In that way, other Christian brothers and sisters can help us see what we're incapable of seeing for ourselves—whether that's pointing out a fruitless branch on the back of our tree or reassuring us that although we're focusing on one bad apple, the overall health of our tree seems good. All this is why the Bible expects Christians to be vitally connected together in local churches. You see, the church is not just a resource-distribution center; it is a group of Christians who help one another walk faithfully in discipleship to Jesus, including in the work of self-examination. The Christian life was never meant to be lived alone, and self-examination should not be done alone either.

Sixth, it is a mistake to let the practical syllogism become the primary source of your assurance.

Throughout this book, we've seen that the driving sources of our spiritual assurance are the gospel of Jesus Christ and the promises of God. By focusing our attention and understanding on these things, we grow in our confidence that Jesus is a powerful Savior—powerful enough to save even sinners like us—and that God will always, infallibly keep his promises to save and preserve those who come to Jesus in faith. If that's true, then self-examination can certainly be *one* thread in the rope of our assurance, but it should never be the primary means or source of it. As human beings, we are bent toward a desire to save ourselves or at least to contribute something to our salvation. Because of that, our hearts are frighteningly adept at taking even something like the fruit of the Spirit and turning them into grounds for pride and self-justification. "Look at all this fruit!" we say. "Now I feel like a Christian!" A true Christian, though—one who understands the moral bankruptcy from which they were saved—will learn the difference between gaining humble encouragement from the fruit they see in their life and taking pride in it (thereby putting faith in it). Faith belongs in Jesus alone and never in our own good works, no matter how bountiful those works might be.

So how do you know if you've subtly begun to make self-examination of your own fruit the primary source of your assurance? There are a few ways to diagnose that problem. One of the most important ways lies in your general sense of spiritual well-being. What is it that most settles your heart and gives you spiritual comfort? Is it meditation on Jesus or reflection on your own life? Do you find that your sense of well-being is mostly or even entirely dependent on how you've "done" this week in avoiding sin or accomplishing spiritual disciplines? If so, then take care. The heart is deceitful and self-righteous above all things, and where it finds the most comfort, there it will put its hope. What a tragedy it would be for you to stand before Jesus with great hope and confidence in all the good works you did in his name and for him to say, "Depart from me, for I never knew you!"

Another indicator that you may be wrongly putting hope in your fruit rather than in Jesus is how you tend to behave when you fall into sin and begin to pursue repentance. According to the logic of the gospel, you ought to begin with finding and embracing forgiveness in Christ and then, out of the strength of hope and forgiveness, proceed to fighting against sin.

Far too many Christians, though, want to run that logic of repentance backward. They think, *First, I have to fix this behavior, and then I will be ready to go to Jesus for forgiveness.* You see the problem with that thinking? It's not much more than salvation by works through the back door—one more way of trying to make ourselves worthy of God's grace and forgiveness. Here's the point: Christians do and must fight against sin, but their *motivation* for that fight is critical. If our motivation is to win God's favor and prove ourselves worthy of his grace, then our fight is not Jesus-glorifying at all but ultimately self-glorifying; it is anti-gospel. A gospel fight against sin, however, launches from a place of forgiveness, acceptance, and love that has already been won for us by Jesus. We don't fight sin to win Jesus's love. We fight sin because we already have Jesus's love.

In the wake of being defeated by sin, what gives you assurance that you can return to Jesus in repentance and find forgiveness and love? Is it that you've cleaned up the mess and recommitted yourself to fighting sin and therefore Jesus will be happy to see you? Or is it simply that Jesus has promised to save sinners—even you—if you come to him in humility and trust?

Conclusion

At various times in history, some Christians have argued that the practical syllogism—that is, the conclusion that we can to some degree confirm our assurance of faith by seeing fruit in our lives, since such fruit is one of the characteristics of a true Christian—is illegitimate precisely because it can look so much like putting faith and hope in one's own good works. But the syllogism doesn't need to be cast aside entirely, and in fact, it can't be if we want to be faithful to the Bible. That's because the Bible *does*, several times, exhort and encourage us to find confirmation of our faith in the fruit that we see growing in our own lives.

That doesn't mean, however, we should launch into that kind of self-examination with abandon. Definite dangers are involved, and those dangers actually lie on both sides—whether we wind up encouraged or discouraged by our introspection. Think about it: If our examination of our good works encourages us, we should be exceedingly careful lest we begin to focus so much on our good works that they become the object of our hope. But there's also the danger that our self-examination can become so obsessive and narrow and exclusive and *dis*couraging that we wind up undermining our sense of assurance entirely.

Despite all those dangers, though, the Bible insists that self-examination is a good and important practice, as long as we keep the cautions we've discussed here carefully in mind. At its best, self-examination can alert us to areas of life that aren't lining up with our profession of faith in Christ. We may see fruitless areas or areas of rotten fruit because we refuse to surrender them to Jesus. We may even begin to recognize a general lack of spiritual health in our lives and be shocked into action by that realization. In those moments, the right course is not to do more good things and fewer bad things. It's to return to the gospel of Jesus Christ and the promises of God, to see his excellencies and be renewed by his love and forgiveness, and then—out of that power and security—renew our fight against sin and for holiness.

On the other hand, our self-examination may actually wind up encouraging us in the faith as we see what God is doing in and through us. We may see acts of love that we know are not natural to us apart from Christ, or renewed vigor in pursuing godliness, or a deepening desire for the things of God. It's not that we would ever hold those good things up as reasons for God to save us, but they may reflexively encourage us to press on even more in the faith, striving to understand more deeply and embrace more tightly the gospel and the promises. The fact is, if you've been tending the root of a tree and suddenly begin to see fruit, it is a right, good, and entirely natural response to be encouraged and then redouble your focus on that root. Used rightly, that's how self-examination ought to work—not as the primary driving source of our assurance but as a confirmation of spiritual health or a warning that it is lacking. Either way, though, the correct response is not to try to increase your assurance by fiddling with the indicator but rather to focus again on the source of both salvation itself and assurance— the gospel of Jesus Christ and the promises of God.

We should address one more knotty problem, though, regarding a particular application of the practical syllogism. Sometimes Christians find themselves repenting over and over again, sometimes even for years, regarding the same sins. And a natural fear is to think, *If I were a real Christian, I wouldn't still be struggling with this sin.* Is that true? How should we think about the sins that just seem to beset us, to dog us no matter how often we repent of them? We turn to that question in the next chapter.

8

What about Besetting Sins?

M y family makes fun of me because one of my favorite movies is *Independence Day*, the one in which Will Smith punches the alien in the downed spaceship and says, "Welcome to Earth!" My movie tastes are decidedly lowbrow, which is probably why *ID4* appeals to me so much. (*ID4* is what its die-hard fans call it; I have no idea why the 4 is there.) At any rate, there are gigantic alien spacecrafts hovering over cities, aerial dogfights between F-15 fighters and alien drones, and famous landmarks being blown to pieces by an alien doomsday weapon. Really, what's not to love?

In one iconic scene, the president of the United States—a young, charismatic former fighter pilot—is holed away in the bunkers of Area 51. When it finally becomes clear that the aliens' goal is the total eradication of humankind, the president gives the colorful order, "Nuke 'em. Let's nuke the scoundrels." (He doesn't actually say "scoundrels," but we'll leave it at that. Google it if you really need to know!)

In response to the president's order, planes scramble and eventually launch a nuclear missile at one of the smaller alien spaceships. There's a massive whiteout explosion and everyone, including the president, waits for word on the result. A communications officer in the bunker asks insistently into a radio transmitter, "Has the target been destroyed?" Finally, after what seems like an eternity, a pilot visually confirms, "Negative. Target remains. I repeat, target remains."[1]

Without a doubt, one of the most urgent questions in many Christians' minds when they begin to think about the topic of assurance is something like this: "But what about this one particular sin that just seems to persist in my life? I hate it. I struggle against it. I repent of it again and again, but the target just . . . remains." Does the presence of persistent sin mean a person is not a Christian? Is that the right conclusion to draw from applying the Bible's practical syllogism?

Right from the beginning, we should acknowledge that the presence of long-persistent sins is a common experience among Christians—so common that it's even earned its own shorthand nickname, "besetting sins," meaning particular sins that continue to plague a Christian over time despite their justification, regeneration, and even ongoing sanctification. Sometimes these besetting sins can even become the defining battle of one's life. Besetting sins take many forms in people's lives. Selfishness, bitterness, anger, lust, gossip, drunkenness, irresponsibility, laziness, worry—all these and more can persist as pitfalls for years in people's lives, causing them to fall over and over again. So, how should we think about these besetting sins, especially given the Bible's teaching that "no one who abides in him keeps on sinning" (1 John 3:6)? I think there is much we can say.

First of all, it's critical to acknowledge that, in one form or another, every Christian has besetting sins. Yes, of course, the particular sins will differ in form, intensity, and even severity of consequences, but every Christian is beset by sin. How exactly can we say that so unequivocally? Because just as clearly as John says that "no one who abides in him keeps on sinning," he also says, "If we say we have no sin, we deceive ourselves, and the truth is not in us" (1:8). Even after we become Christians, our sin nature remains. Yes, we are set free from the condemnation of sin and its slavery, but the battle between the flesh and the Spirit remains. That's Paul's point in Galatians 5:16–25. As Christians, we will always be tempted to live according to the flesh, but our call is to continue to fight to "walk by the Spirit" (v. 16) and "keep in step with the Spirit" (v. 25).

One of the most arresting images Paul uses in that passage is the call for those who believe in Christ to crucify "the flesh with its passions and desires" (v. 24). The image is striking because it implies that we ought to strive to carry on violent, no-holds-barred war against our sin. Yet at the same time, it reminds us of the ongoing nature of that warfare; it will not end quickly or easily. I love how one pastor described the continuing act of crucifying the flesh:

> Crucifixion . . . produced death not suddenly but gradually. . . . True Christians do not succeed in completely destroying it (that is the flesh) while here below; but they have fixed it to the cross and they are determined to keep it there till it expires.[2]

The slow crucifixion of the flesh is not the special burden of a few unfortunate or weak Christians. It's the call and responsibility of *every* Christian. To be sure, not every Christian's fight is the same. Sin has colored us all in a thousand awful ways. For some, the ongoing struggle will be against visible, outward behaviors; for others, it will be against hellish attitudes of the heart. For some, the enemies will come rank upon rank for a lifetime; others will be locked in mortal combat against a single enemy for a lifetime. The important point is to recognize that we as Christians will not be completely freed of sin and its effects until we stand with Jesus. In fact, it seems to be the unbroken expectation of the Bible that until that day, and in one way or another, we will all wrestle with sin (see Prov. 20:9; Matt. 6:12–14; Rom. 7:21–25; Gal. 5:17; James 3:2; 1 John 1:8–10).

Second, the presence of besetting sins does not necessarily call into question our salvation. Of course, it could, and we'll discuss those particular circumstances shortly, but it's important to remember that John himself recognized that we will repeatedly sin and repeatedly return to the Savior for forgiveness. "If we confess our sins," he writes, "he is faithful and just to forgive us" (1 John 1:9).

Even more, Jesus himself seemed to recognize that confession of sin is not a one-and-done proposition. In Matthew 18, Peter asks Jesus how many times he should forgive his brother for sinning against him. At first glance, Peter's initial suggestion seems reasonable, if not generous: "As many as seven times?" he asks. But Jesus's answer is nothing short of astonishing: "Jesus said to him, 'I do not say to you seven times, but seventy-seven times'" (vv. 21–22). Don't sell him short though! Jesus is not saying you get seventy-seven chances, but seventy-eight is a bridge too far. The numbers are symbolic—seven being the number of completeness and ten of totality. So Jesus's answer is actually, "Well, what is completeness *times* totality *plus* another completeness? Whatever it is, you should forgive *that* many times." The real encouragement from that exchange with Peter, though, is in the reason Jesus gives for why we ourselves should be unendingly forgiving. It's because God has forgiven us infinitely more even than that!

The point from both John's and Jesus's teachings is that God seems to know and expect that sin will drive us again and again to the Savior for forgiveness. In fact, that may be part of the reason why God doesn't simply glorify us and free us from all temptation the instant we become Christians. You realize he could have done that, right? In fact, he *will* do that the moment we either die or rise to meet Christ in the air. "In a moment," Paul writes, "in the twinkling of an eye . . . we shall be changed" (1 Cor. 15:52). So, if God can make it happen, then why doesn't he do it the moment we're converted? Why does he allow us to go on struggling with sin instead of glorifying us immediately? The bottom line is that we probably can't know all his reasons, but one is surely so that we may learn more and more deeply how to depend on Jesus for life and salvation. And the fact is that the sins with which we struggle the most, and the temptations that continue to entice us most alluringly throughout our lives, often prove to be some of the things that drive us most strongly to despair of self and to trust in Christ. It's just as Paul writes at the end of Romans 7: "Wretched man that I am! Who will deliver me from this body of death? Thanks be to God through Jesus Christ our Lord" (vv. 24–25).

Third, we must ask to what degree we should expect to achieve victory over besetting sins in this life. Some have

131

argued that we should expect total victory over every besetting sin; we should expect it in this life; and if a person
doesn't experience that kind of victory, then they cannot
possibly be a true Christian. But given even what we've discussed in the first two sections of this chapter, that seems
to suggest quite a bit more than the Bible actually promises.
The ultimate answer to the questions "How much victory
should I expect?" or "How much maturity should I expect?"
is that it is all in God's hands. In Hebrews 6:1, the author exhorts his readers to leave the elementary teachings of Christ
and "go on to maturity," a goal we would think would be
within God's will, no question. But then in verse 3, he makes
this cryptic remark: "And this we will do *if God permits*"
(emphasis added). What a strange thing to say! Does that
mean God might *not* permit these believers to press on to
maturity? Well, yes, and that shouldn't be entirely surprising
to Christians. Our salvation, our growth, our sanctification,
our maturity, even our victory over sin are ultimately in his
sovereign hands.

The fact is, there is no promise in the Bible of total victory
over sin in our lives—even over any particular sin—until we
stand in glory with Christ. But even so, it seems reasonable
to think we should have a *general* expectation—though not
a watertight guarantee—of some degree of victory over sin.
And we certainly should strive and pray for that kind of victory. That's Paul's point when he writes that because you
have been crucified and resurrected with Christ, you should

let not sin therefore reign in your mortal body, to make you
obey its passions. Do not present your members to sin as
instruments for unrighteousness, but present yourselves to

God as those who have been brought from death to life, and your members to God as instruments for righteousness. For sin will have no dominion over you, since you are not under law but under grace. (Rom. 6:12–14)

Paul's point is not that we will always win in our battle against sin but that we are free now to fight it and not simply obey it. We are no longer slaves; we are warriors. So, the general expectation would seem to be that we will see *some* degree of increased victory, and at least periods of victory, as our love for Christ deepens and our ability to stand firm against temptation therefore increases. At the very least, with any particular sin, we can be confident that a true Christian will not be consumed by it. At some point, the God who will not lose a single one of those whom he has given to his Son will say to the destroying waters of sin, "Thus far shall you come, and no farther" (Job 38:11).

Fourth, we should ask at what point any particular persistent sin should cause a Christian to fear for their salvation. The presence of a besetting sin should cause genuine alarm in two situations. The first is when the reality is not that you are struggling with a narrow streak of sin in the tapestry of a life that is otherwise marked by love for God and growth in Christ, but rather you are staring at a pattern of sin that has become the dominant character of your life. When your besetting sins have grown to the point that your affections, plans, thoughts, emotions, actions, and words are determined and shaped by those sins, they have become dangerous—a genuine threat to the credibility of your profession of faith.

The second circumstance that should cause alarm is when your besetting sins have ceased to bother you—when your heart has made peace with those sins and even longs for them, finds comfort in them, justifies them, and no longer rises up in rebellion against them. The point is, you can't simply categorize a sin in your life as "besetting" and declare that it therefore doesn't matter anymore or that you're somehow excused from fighting it. "Well, this is just my besetting sin" is not an excuse not to fight. In fact, such a response might well be more like the response of a child of the darkness than a child of the light.

When it comes to any sin—whether one that's easily beaten or one that requires a lifetime of warfare—the critical issue is not the behavior itself (after all, not all sins are behaviors at all) but rather how your heart responds to it. I love how one writer beautifully puts this truth:

> The difference between an unconverted and a converted man is not that the one has sins and the other has none; but that the one takes part with his cherished sins against a dreaded God, and the other takes part with a reconciled God against his hated sins.[3]

Ultimately, this is the critical question: Have you surrendered to sin, or are you fighting it? The fact is, I would have far more confidence in the true faith of a person who is wholeheartedly fighting a battle with heinous visible sin, regularly losing, and each time crying out to Christ for mercy than I would in a person who has given up on fighting even the smallest, most invisible peccadillo. The former person is a warrior who has said to sin, "You may beat me over and over, but I have a new King now, and for his sake I will never live at peace with you again!" And the other? They have knelt at sin's feet.

You see, the call to fight is a call to every Christian, whether or not they can identify a particular persistent sin in their life. The important thing in the war against sin is not so much to see victory; that will come in due time, when God permits. For now, the important thing is to make sure you can see the smoke of battle. There's the question: When you look at your own sin, persistent or not, do you see the smoke of battle? And if not, why not?

Fifth and finally, what should you do with the sin that persists in your life? I think there are two kinds of people we must address here. Perhaps you're a Christian who is in the midst of a smoky battle against your sin—tempted, torn, tried, weary, worn, and tired—and yet clinging to Jesus for mercy with all your might and doing everything you can to resist sin and war against it. To you, the message is simple: be encouraged and keep fighting! You are not alone in having to fight against sin; that's exactly what the Bible tells us to expect. After all, a declaration of faith in Jesus is a declaration of war against hell. And guess what happens when you declare war against hell and sin? It declares war right back. Besides, the very mark of a Christian with regard to sin is that they will keep fighting, keep wrestling and striving, keep running the race set before them. And that's exactly what you're doing. Listen, your battle with sin will not last forever, and the Bible's promise is that you *will* outlast your sin. You will live to see it pulled from your heart by the roots and vanquished. It will take its last breath as you take your first in the bright air of eternity. Live and fight and trust Christ for that day.

But perhaps you're the other kind of person, the kind who is in fact not in the midst of a struggle against sin. It's not that you've defeated it; it's that you've surrendered to it. Perhaps, even by reading parts of this book, you've been shocked into realizing that your lack of assurance is entirely warranted because it's caused by the fact that you are living like a child of the darkness. Sin has become the dominant color on your canvas. If that's your situation, then what you need to do is simple: repent. Agree with God about the evil of your sin, and repent. Repentance is not just a matter of emotion or of stopping some behavior. It's a matter of doing everything necessary to embrace the beauty of Christ and learning to love him more than you love your sin.

In the end, when it comes to persistent sin in our lives, there's no flowchart to follow, as if we could answer six questions and have a diagnosis and prescription in hand. As Christians, we must fight sin with constant vigilance and constant awareness that we are not home yet. We should also constantly remind our hearts that our hope for eternity doesn't rest in our attaining perfection but rather in our knowing that Jesus attained perfection *for* us and won our salvation. In our fight against sin, we're always faced with two pitfalls. One is obvious. It is to stop caring about it, to be defeated by it, to give in to it and sink into the darkness. But the other is evil in its subtlety and just as deadly. It is to make perfection or even victory an idol, to foolishly put our trust in our own sin-fighting prowess rather than in the Savior and to think that one day we will stand before God and say, "I beat it. That's why you should accept me!" As Christians, we must be vigilant not to fall into either of those traps. Rather, we must be aware of our sin, let it drive us to Christ and his gospel, and then let his love for us and our love for him motivate us in our resistance to sin until he glorifies us in his presence on the last day.

Finally, it's crucial to understand that our fight as Christians is not only *against* something but also *for* something. We don't just fight against the horror of sin; we fight for the glories of eternity. For all its notoriety as a book that frightens Christians, 1 John is actually chock-full of encouragements to Christians about what they are fighting *for*, not just what they are fighting against. For example, in 1 John 2:28, John holds out to us the prospect that we can have confidence about the coming of Jesus. We don't have to dread it as a day of shame and uncovering; instead, we can look forward to it as redeemed people whose sins have been cast into a bottomless sea. We needn't shrink from that day, but rather we should strain forward to reach it, knowing that when Jesus returns, our struggle with sin will be finished once and for all and we will finally be able to rest.

John also encourages us to rejoice in our adoption as children of God. He writes, "See what kind of love the Father has given to us, that we should be called children of God; and so we are" (1 John 3:1). That verse really should contain more exclamation points, because John is writing with astonished exultation. "Look at this!" he is saying. "Can you believe it?! What kind of love is it that would take sinners like us and make us children of God?" This doctrine of adoption must be one of the most precious and unexpected truths in the entire Bible. Why? Because God could have saved us by doing so much *less* than that. He could have forgiven us, made us servants, given us the rank of the angels, *anything*—and the universe would have stood astonished at his mercy. But he did more than all of that. He made us sons and daughters. He put robes on our shoulders and rings on our fingers and embraced us and welcomed us home. That's why we fight—not just because sin is our mortal enemy, but because God is our Father. We fight as sons and daughters of the King.

Last, John encourages us to look forward to the day when we will be like Jesus: "Beloved, we are God's children now, and what we will be has not yet appeared; but we know that when he appears we shall be like him, because we shall see him as he is" (v. 2). That has been the goal since the very beginning; it is what God predestined for you as one he foreloved—"to be conformed to the image of his Son" (Rom. 8:29). Take heart in knowing that God's purposes will never fail. The day is coming when your struggle against sin, your exhausting resistance against the world and the flesh and the devil will end. The day is coming when you will be like Jesus.

I once had a poster hanging in my office that depicted a sculpture. At first glance, it looked like a crystal man, his arms stretched up to heaven, being swallowed from below by some sinister, gray-colored mud creeping up his legs. But at the bottom of the poster were printed the words from 1 John 3:2: "What we will be has not yet appeared." You see, the crystal man wasn't being swallowed by his sin; he was escaping it. He was being pulled out of it. Against all odds, he was being glorified and made like Christ. Dear Christian, the day is coming when God will extract you from the battle, remove sin once and for all from your heart, and set you on high with Christ. Until then, keep fighting. Keep resisting. Keep loving. And above all, keep setting your eyes on Jesus.

Striving for Assurance

One of the most enjoyable parts of my trip to Mount Everest was spending time with my two Sherpa guides, Samdan and Hira. Hira was a twenty-six-year-old guy who served as a porter, meaning that it was his job to hoist a forty-pound bag full of my gear on his back every day and schlep it up the mountain. Believe it or not, bearing that kind of weight isn't unusual for Sherpas in the Himalayas. From a very young age, many of them spend their days carrying jaw-droppingly large loads up and down the mountain paths. Hira was training to be a guide, but it would be probably another five years before he would get his first shot at it. In the meantime, it was his job to carry the luggage—and to learn English, which is a necessary skill if you're going to be a successful guide. Throughout the trip, Hira would pick up on various phrases I used and walk behind me on the trail practicing them over and over again, trying to get the inflection just right. "What's up, what's *up*, *what's* up, whatsup, up's what!"

Samdan, however, was no trainee. An undisputed expert of the trail and experienced trek guide, he told me at one point that in twenty years of guiding trips like mine, he had made over two hundred treks to Base Camp. His greatest dream was to be hired one day to take someone to the summit. "You maybe?" he asked once. "Absolutely not!" I replied.

The trek wasn't easy. Oh, there was nothing technical about it—no crampons or ropes or any particular skill needed. But eventually, the altitude became a problem, and by the time we strolled into Base Camp at 17,700 feet above sea level, I was huffing and puffing to catch my breath and fighting a nasty headache. The highest we went on the trek was 18,200 feet to the summit of a little foothill called Kala Patthar, which is said to have the most magnificent views of Everest in the world, especially if you can get there before the sun rises. So, at 3:30 a.m. on the last day of climbing, we started up the ascent of Kala Patthar. That name, *Kala Patthar*, is Nepalese for "black rock." It's a perfect name—and not at all creative, it turns out—because the little foothill is actually made up of billions of little black pebbles piled up in such a way that it looks like someone did it on purpose. Again, there's nothing particularly difficult about climbing Kala Patthar. At sea level, you could probably jog up it in half an hour or so, maybe less. But at 18,000 feet and half the oxygen you're used to at sea level, it's a slog. You take a step, breathe for three or four seconds, then take another step. Then you do that same thing a few thousand more times. And behind you, in all their splendor, are the Himalayas spread out in speech-defying beauty, their summits one by one being crowned with the gold of the rising sun.

I was tired though. And yet I was also trying to remain upbeat and keep conversation going with Samdan. I started asking him questions, attempting to make small talk. "Where did these black rocks come from?" I asked.

"I do not know," he replied.

"Well, what do you think they're made of?"

"Really, I do not know."

"How many of them do you think there are? Why are they black anyway?"

Finally, with a smile but also a puzzled look, Samdan turned around and swept his arms across the mountains. "Mister Greg," he said, "all this . . . why do you keep looking at the pebbles?"

What a question, right? And not just about mountain climbing either. It's just as poignant when applied to our spiritual lives: Why do we as Christians spend so much of our time focusing on the pebbles rather than on the glittering mountain range of promises God has made to us in Christ? The fact is, much of our struggle to feel assured of God's love for us—and therefore our security in salvation—is the result of having too crabbed, narrow, and small a vision. As we conclude this book, therefore, let's think about some of the "pebbles" we tend to look at instead of taking in the breathtaking views of God's promises and the gospel.

Pebble #1: We Focus on Ourselves Rather Than the Gospel and the Promises

If you take any idea away from this book, let it be this: you will never deepen your faith in Jesus—and therefore strengthen your confidence and assurance of your salvation—by staring at yourself all the time. The fountainhead and bottomless well of assurance is the utterly trustworthy and completely inexhaustible truth that Jesus has loved and acted to save sinners and that God has promised and sworn by his own infinite self that his Son's mission to save sinners will not fail—not even in the smallest particular. Get your mind around that, plant your heart in that soil, and you will find your assurance growing and strengthening. The more trustworthy and faithful you learn God to be, the more you will trust him and the more certain you will be in that trust.

What this means, in the most practical terms, is that you need to take specific action to remove your eyes from yourself and plant them on God. Read books about God, about theology, about who God is and what he has done, and read them for God's own sake—to know him and love him and stand in awe of him—not just for the sake of figuring out what "applicational nugget" you can walk away with. Meditate on God's trinitarian nature, even if you can't see an immediate application. Dwell on the intricacies of sacrifices and atonement, even if those details don't seem immediately "relevant." As you broaden your vision of God, you will find your love and awe of him deepening. And the result will be that you will trust him more. Your certainty that he will move heaven and earth to keep his promises will solidify. Even more, make sure you are a vital, contributing member of a local church. Gather with brothers and sisters who are themselves engaged in the fight, sing hymns of praise to God, hear his Word read and preached, lift up your voice with them in prayer. What you will find is that fellowship with other believers will remind you of God's promises, spiritually stabilize you, and reinvigorate you to continue the fight.

Often the very best way to deepen our assurance of salvation is to peel our eyes off ourselves entirely and put them on God and his people.

When you really begin to think about it, what foolishness it is to believe that the way to deepen our trust in God is to focus on ourselves! In the end and at its essence, the search for assurance is the search for a firm place to stand, a floor of bedrock that will not move and on which we can begin to build. And the fact is, we will never find that bedrock by looking at and thinking about ourselves. What we will find in our own hearts is weakness and vacillation, but he is the same yesterday, today, and forever. What we will see in ourselves is a ship thrown to and fro by the waves, but he is the Rock of Ages, forever immovable. What we will find in our hearts is fear and doubt, but he holds the keys of death and Hades. Look to him, not yourself, and let your heart find rest.

Pebble #2: We Focus on the Abstract Rather Than the Concrete

One of the most dangerous things a Christian can do is lose sight of the fact that Christianity is not an ephemeral religion. It's not primarily an ethical system or a philosophical school of thought. At its heart, it's not even primarily about ideas, though it certainly has plenty of those. Ultimately, the sine qua non of Christianity is its declaration that certain events happened in history. Jesus came, lived, died, and rose again—really, in history, and all of it happened just as surely and concretely as any other historical event in the history of the world. When we Christians say those things *happened*, we're not speaking metaphorically or narratively or "spiritually." We mean it! And therefore being a Christian begins with believing those historical facts and then believing what Jesus himself said about the significance of those events. Christianity is concrete, objective, and *graspable*, not abstract and inscrutable.

When it comes to questions of assurance, though, so many Christians get lost in a vortex of abstractions. What's the philosophical nature of faith? What does it mean to believe that you believe or to trust that you're trusting? Can there be quantities of faith or different textures of believing? Is my joy strong enough? To be sure, some of those are interesting questions, and there's a place for them. But that place is not in the rubble of a Christian heart whose faith and assurance are collapsing. When that happens, what you need is bedrock, not clouds. Concreteness, not abstraction.

One of the most useful practices I've found for settling my faith and sense of assurance is to go right back to the foundation of my faith by asking myself (and answering) the very first questions. Doing so has the effect of planting my feet on the rock again and allowing me to build up from there. So, for example, when you feel your faith is failing, start like this and answer honestly:

Do I believe there is a God? *Yes, I do.*

Do I believe Jesus of Nazareth really existed? *Yes, I do.*

Do I believe he is the Son of God? *You know what? I do. I really do.*

Do I believe he died on the cross? *Yes.*

Do I believe that when he died, he was dying in the place of sinners? *Yes.*

144

Do I believe he really, truly, bodily rose from the dead? *I do. Against all odds, I actually do!*

Do I believe I am a sinner who needs to be saved? *Yes.*

Do I believe Jesus when he said everyone who trusts in him will not perish? *Yes.*

Do I believe God when he said everyone who calls on the name of the Lord will be saved? *Yes, yes, yes.*

You see? As you ask questions like those, you can actually ground your faith in the concrete truths of who Jesus is, what he did, and what he promised. You can build it from the ground up and feel it strengthening as you answer "yes, yes, yes" again and again. And what if you run into a question to which you can't answer yes? Then keep asking questions. Why do I hesitate to answer yes to that particular question? Is it because I can't quite believe Jesus rose from the dead? Is it because I harbor an idea that God may save others, but I am too far gone? Sometimes chasing down the answer to why you can't answer yes will uncover a deep-rooted problem that, once identified, you can address clearly and directly.

If you struggle with assurance of salvation, don't spend any more time swimming around in abstractions. Take your lack of assurance to the source. Interrogate yourself and find out what you believe without hesitation, identify the precise point at which your faith starts to falter, and build from there. Certainty isn't found in abstractions. It's found in the concrete realities of the life, death, and resurrection of Jesus, as well as in the promise of God to save those who trust in him.

Pebble #3: We Focus on Our Individual Spiritual Lives Rather Than the Life of the Church

Sometimes we tend to focus on our individual spiritual lives instead of the life of the church. This is not at all to say it's *wrong* to focus on our own individual spiritual growth. It's not. But at the same time, it's important to realize that again and again the Bible makes it clear that spiritual growth is meant to happen—indeed, is *designed by God* to happen—in the context of a local church. That's especially true when it comes to the work of self-examination and the strengthening of assurance. And it's true for at least a couple of reasons.

For one thing, we simply can't see our own lives clearly enough to render a judgment about them. Our deceitful hearts will inevitably either focus inordinately on the rotten fruit in our lives or overlook it entirely. Because of that, part of the very purpose of the church—the reason Jesus established it in the first place—is to provide an outside judgment about whether we are living the kind of life that renders our profession of faith in Christ credible. Think about the man who is put out of the fellowship of the church in 1 Corinthians 5. The reason Paul told the church to take that action was because the man's unrepentant behavior was "not tolerated even among pagans" (v. 1) and therefore it was inconsistent with a credible profession of trust in Christ. That's a tragic situation, but think about the reverse. When a church agrees to bring a person into its membership (as long as they actually take that kind of decision seriously), they are essentially saying, "Yes, your understanding of the gospel is correct, and as far as we can tell from your life, we think you really are a Christian." In that way, the members of a church are actually locking arms and offering mutual reassurance to one another that they are in fact fellow believers in Jesus.

That's the formal way being a member of a church helps, but even informally, we simply *need* other believers to help us see ourselves clearly. We need other Christians around us who can say, "I know you're struggling with that sin, sister. But look how God is working in your life in this area and that area. Joy may be a fight for you right now, but my goodness the Lord is producing the fruit of patience in you!" However, we also need other believers sometimes to say, "Brother, I know you think you're doing well spiritually, but it's created a really noticeable streak of pride in you lately. You should watch out for that." And sometimes it can simply be a matter of a Christian brother or sister saying, "Enough about you! We've talked about you for an hour, man. Enough introspection! Let's think about Jesus now." The point is, abiding in fellowship with other believers by being a vital, living member of a church is not optional to a healthy sense of spiritual assurance. It's key to having a right view of ourselves and therefore a strong and well-founded assurance.

One more point: we've said throughout this book that the presence of the fruit of the Spirit is one of the means God uses to confirm us in our assurance. But have you ever noticed how those fruits simply don't make sense without other believers around? Love, joy, peace, patience, kindness, goodness, faithfulness, gentleness, self-control—those virtues simply won't grow and mature without other people around. Think about each of them and try to imagine them growing and strengthening in a solitary life. It won't happen! But when we commit ourselves to living life with other believers—through the ups and downs, good times and bad—we'll create an environment where love, patience, kindness, gentleness, self-control, and all the rest of those fruits will have the opportunity to flourish.

Jesus Loves Me, This I *Know*

I hope that in the course of reading this book, dear friend, you've come to a few clear realizations. The first is that Christian confidence and assurance are not things God intends for just *some* Christians, much less the *best* ones. Throughout the Bible, the general expectation is that our hearts will be firmly settled in the knowledge that we have been made sons and daughters of God and that we are therefore heirs of eternal life. If you are a Christian, then God *intends* for you not to be racked by fear and doubt but to be able to rest in the arms of your Savior as you trust him to bring you safely home.

I also hope you've realized that Christian assurance is not some unfathomable mystery or inscrutable spiritual alchemy. The Bible gives us very clear direction on how to strengthen our faith and assurance—that is, first, by deepening our understanding of and tightening our embrace on the gospel and the divine promises, and second, by carefully and rightly examining our lives to see and be encouraged by the fruit of the Spirit's work in us. Give yourself to pursuing those things, in that order, and your faith will strengthen; and as it does, your assurance will do the same. And even then, sometimes the clouds will part and you will see by the Spirit more clearly than ever what you already knew to be true—that Jesus loves sinners and that God has promised to save all those who trust in him.

148

Ultimately, to be assured in your faith is not a complicated matter. It's simply to know beyond a shadow of a doubt that the most important things are indeed true. And more often than not, the most important things are also the simplest. A story is told of a man in the 1960s who had developed a reputation as one of the greatest theologians of the twentieth century. He wrote massive, learned books and gave lectures all over the world, and though he was not finally right in all his conclusions, he was never accused of thinking small thoughts about God. Once, when he had concluded a series of lectures at a university in Chicago, a member of the audience rose to ask him a question. "Sir, what is the greatest thought that has ever crossed your mind?" The theologian bowed his head and paused for a long moment, his fingers pressed together under his chin, and considered his answer. Then he raised his eyes and said quietly, "Jesus loves me, this I *know*. For the Bible tells me so."

In the end, there's no simpler thought than that. And yet, at the same time, no greater truth has ever rung through the cosmos. God so loved the world that he gave his one and only Son, that whoever believes in him should not perish but have eternal life.

Even if all else should give way and fail, and the earth itself were removed from its foundation, of *that* we can be assured!

Notes

Chapter 2 The Driving Sources of Assurance: The Gospel of Jesus
Christ

1. Martin Luther, *Works* (Weimar, 1883), 5:608.

2. *English Oxford Living Dictionaries*, s.v. "faith," accessed August
23, 2018, https://en.oxforddictionaries.com/definition/faith.

Chapter 3 The Driving Sources of Assurance: The Promises of God

1. Ada Ruth Habershon and Matthew Merker, "He Will Hold Me
Fast" (1906).

Chapter 4 The Supernatural Source of Assurance: The Witness of
the Spirit

1. See also Ephesians 4:30 and 2 Corinthians 1:22.

2. Benjamin B. Warfield, *Faith and Life* (New York: Longmans, 1916),
191.

Chapter 5 The Undermining of Assurance: The Lies We Believe

1. John Owen, *On Communion with God* (1657), *Works* 2:32.

2. Owen, *On Communion with God*.

3. Sinclair Ferguson, *The Whole Christ: Legalism, Antinomianism,
and Gospel Assurance—Why the Marrow Controversy Still Matters*
(Wheaton: Crossway, 2016), 69.

4. Ferguson, *The Whole Christ*, 69.

5. Ira Stanphill, "Mansion over the Hilltop" (1949).

Chapter 6 The Confirming Source of Assurance: The Fruits of Obedience

1. Robert Murray McCheyne and Andrew Bonar, "The Life and Remains, Letters, Lectures, and Poems of the Rev. Robert Murray McCheyne" (New York: Robert Carter and Brothers, 1866), 220, https://books.google.com/books?id=jvMsAAAAYAAJ&pg=PA220&dq=For+every+look+at+yourself,+take+ten+looks+at+Christ&hl=en&sa=X&ved=0ahUKEwju38vwhpXdAhVFmlkKHZxAA8IQ6AEIMTAB#v=onepage&q=For%20every%20look%20at%20yourself%2C%20take%20ten%20looks%20at%20Christ&f=false.

Chapter 7 Misusing a Good Tool: Mistakes We Make in Considering Our Good Works

1. Google Dictionary, s.v. "syllogism," accessed October 15, 2018, https://www.google.com/search?q=syllogism&oq=syllogism&aqs=chrome..69i57j0l5.266j0j7&sourceid=chrome&ie=UTF-8.

Chapter 8 What about Besetting Sins?

1. *Independence Day*, directed by Roland Emmerich (Los Angeles, CA: Twentieth Century Fox, 1996).

2. John Stott, *The Message of Galatians* (Downers Grove, IL: InterVarsity, 1984), xx.

3. William Arnot, *Laws from Heaven for Life on Earth* (London: T. Nelson and Sons, 1884), 311.

Greg Gilbert (MDiv, Southern Seminary) is senior pastor of Third Avenue Baptist Church in downtown Louisville, Kentucky. He lives in Kentucky with his wife, Moriah, and their three children, where he enjoys basketball, coffee, and Thai food.

ALSO AVAILABLE
FROM GREG GILBERT

Many Christians are under the mistaken impression that while God's grace may be a gift, his favor is something we must earn. This misunderstanding leads ultimately to lives that feel unfulfilled and inadequate. Pastor Greg Gilbert puts favor back in its rightful place, as God's gift through Jesus Christ. He shows how the favor Jesus earned through his perfect life and sacrificial death becomes ours the moment we believe. Knowing we already have God's favor frees us to live joyous lives no matter our physical or material circumstances.

Printed in Great Britain
by Amazon

17458577R00093